TRUST YOUR HUSTLE PT. 1

"A LIFE FORGED BY FIRE"

Anthony Trucks

Books may be purchased in quantity and/or special sales by contacting the
Author, Anthony Trucks, at 1705 Yellowstone Dr Antioch CA 94509,
925-756-7321, or by email at contact@anthonytrucks.com

Published by: Anthony Trucks Industries, LLC
Interior Design by: Vanessa Maynard
Cover Design by: Vanessa Maynard
Editing by: Judi Blaze

Anthony, Trucks, 2014 – Trust Your Hustle Pt 1: A life forged by fire
First printing - 2014
ISBN: 978-1502721990
ISBN-10: 1502721996
1413121110 9 8 7 6 5 4 3 2 1
First Edition
Printed in America
www.AnthonyTrucks.com

TABLE OF CONTENTS

ACKNOWLEDGMENTS

There are more people to thank than I can imagine I will be able to remember, but I will do my best. First of all I would like to thank God for brining me into this world and allowing me the ability to experience all that I have on this planet. My mom, who recently passed, for raising me to be the man I am today. My Dad for being superman, and one of my greatest supporters in all that I do. My very wise older brother for being a great example of how a Christian man should treat his family, and the people in his life. My half blood siblings for always being a driving force to make you all proud.

Thanks to my best friend in the world for being the mental ying to my yang and keeping me sane through life's troubles since we met in the 4th grade. My grandparents, aunts, and uncles for loving me without fail. My in-laws for being some of my greatest supporters and loving me unconditionally. Jeff, Anthony, Jerry, Byron, Khristian, Jamar, Scott, Kyree, Ed, and Dan for being part of my close circle and my strength & direction when I needed you all the most. Thanks to my college coaches for giving me the blessing of my future and teaching me to be a great man, teammate, and leader.

Special thanks to all of my employees/coworkers/friends over the years for supporting me as their "flawed' leader, and helping me achieve my dream of helping others. Thanks to Todd Durkin and Larry for being my guiding lights through very dark times. I respect you men more than you'll ever know. Every client I have ever worked with and have befriended, because you gave me some of the fondest memories I will ever have in this life. I gained more from every session with you all, whether I trained you personally or not, than you may ever comprehend because you all taught me how to truly treat people the way I want to be treated in all aspects of life.

Last but not least, my ex-wife for some truly amazing years. Although life has its way of redirecting paths, I no know nothing that happened in our lives together was a negative, because positives blossomed from the roots of all our tragedies.

DEDICATION

I want to dedicate this book to 5 people. The first three are my children who literally ARE my heart. I have wanted nothing more in my life than to raise my own happy and healthy children so that I can give them the world I missed out on. I spend my days thinking of how I can make sure that when I send my children out into the world they are more than equipped to handle it. I want to do that by my words and, more importantly, my actions. That way I can be sure that I have given my kids all the love, support, and examples a father can give a child, as well as the tools to duplicate that love, support, and life examples for their own children; my highly anticipated grandchildren. If I could choose for one thing to come of this book it would be that my kids and grandkids would be able to know and respect me for the man I was long after my vessel has left the earth.

The fourth is my dad. You took me in as your own at the age of 20 and loved me like your own flesh and blood. I will never be able to repay you for all that you have done for me and our family over the years as you raised us all while taking care of our sick mom, your wife. You are the best example of a loving husband that the world may ever see. You raised us like a champ while you raised yourself in the process.

Last but so far from least, my mom. You are no longer with me physically, but you will live on through me every day in all that I do. Every person I reach and help in my life will be because of the unconditional love you showed a young bad child when he was 6 years old. You taught me how to love in more ways than one when I hated the world. This book is dedicated to your memory and I wouldn't have it any other way. I just pray God allows me to succeed in my goal of helping as many people as possible feel the unconditional love you gave me.

FOREWORD

I believe all of us have a life worth telling a story about. And the deeper the story, the more profound a difference one can make in other people's lives.

That being said, many of us have faced much adversity, heartache, and challenge in life. Sometimes life seems too busy, too overwhelming, and downright defeating.

And I have always said that adversity and challenge can do one of a few things to you:

1. *It can knock you down, keep you down, and spiral you into a deep, dark place.*
2. *It can propel you forward by you ultimately choosing to DO SOMETHING positive with your life.*
3. *Or it can do both!*

As a performance coach, trainer, speaker, and business owner, I have had the opportunity to work with many "high level" athletes and executives. From NFL MVP's, Super Bowl champions & MVP's, MLB & NBA All-Stars, and Olympic Gold Medalists to the uber-successful entrepreneur that is worth billions of dollars. Literally.

And one thing is common with the great ones. All the ones I know and have worked with have overcome some form of massive adversity in their life. Major injury. Disease. Bankruptcy. Divorce. Tragedy in the family. Horrible childhood. Failed businesses. And the list goes on and on.

Now I am NOT saying you have to experience these to be successful in life. You don't.

But here is the bottom line. "Good things" and "bad things" are going happen in life. And there are some things you can control and there are some things you can't control.

And a mantra I live by is, "It's not what happens TO us in life that counts. It's what we choose to DO with it that matters most."

Let me introduce to you Mr. Anthony Trucks. I first met Anthony in April 2010 at a 3.5 Day Mentorship that I host annually for fitness professionals. Amongst the 30 or so other attendees at this intensive event meant to dive deep into business and personal development, Anthony immediately stood out.

He was built like an Adonis. Big strapping muscles. Confident posture. Well-groomed. He looked like he could suit up and play in an NFL game next week.

Anthony was also soft-spoken. Respectful. Humble. Approachable. And friendly.

But what I didn't know at the time was Anthony's story. Woaahhh.

I didn't know that he grew up in the foster care system.

I didn't know that he was passed around from family to family.

I didn't know that he was beaten and abused as a child.

I didn't know sports saved him from going down a dark road.

I didn't know that he earned a football scholarship to the
*   University of Oregon.*

I didn't know he had a child before graduating college.

I didn't know he went through a long-winding journey to
*   ultimately fulfill his dream of playing in the NFL.*

I didn't know he went through an ugly divorce.

I didn't know he had a failed business.

And I certainly didn't know the incredible drive and determination this man had to make such a huge positive impact in the world.

I just knew that this one fateful April afternoon when I met Anthony that he was an eager young 25 year-old man ready to learn. And that he was hungry for success. And that he was willing to do whatever it took to get there.

Over the last few years, I have gotten to know Anthony and see him grow. And I've gotten to learn his story.

A pastor mentor of mine, Miles McPherson, once told me, "If you think you have problems, just go find someone else with bigger problems. Because they are all around you!"

In Anthony's "Trust Your Hustle" book, I couldn't believe what this man had to endure as a child. NO ONE human being should ever have to experience and endure what he did. And the challenges and strife that he has faced throughout his life would break most men and women.

Yet for Anthony, it has only forged him to become WHO he is today. A man of faith. A man of conviction. A man of determination. A man of action. A man of HUSTLE.

He's a father. A coach. A trainer. A speaker. A businessman. And now an author.

I'm so proud and happy that Anthony decided to share his story. While probably not easy to share some of what you are about to read in the following pages, there is no doubt you are going to experience just some of the positive emotions that I felt:

Hope. *Hope for the future and all that is to be.*

Motivated. *Motivated to be a better parent. A better spouse.*

A better person.

Convicted. *Convicted to do what is right in life. Period.*

Inspired. *Inspired to help more people. Regardless of where* *you are in life right now, you can always help more*

people. And that servant-hood attitude to human-kind is

wanted and needed.

Grateful. *Grateful and blessed for what and WHO is IN our lives.*

My friend, this book will give you perspective about life. And if you ever think you have/had it bad, just realize what Anthony has overcome. It could always be worse.

When I say that "Everyone has a life worth telling a story about...what's your story?"™, I mean it. It is true. Every ONE has a life worth telling a story about. But it's up to you to CHOOSE to do something extraordinary with your life.

And the more adversity and challenge you have faced in the past or that you are facing now, the more people you can ultimately influence and impact. But you must be willing to act and to overcome.

Anthony, from the bottom of my heart, thank you for having the courage to overcome. To never give-up. To keep on pressing and believing. And I thank you for sharing your story. It has not only made me a better person, I am confident that is going to motivate, inspire and IMPACT thousands of other people as well.

As I conclude, please remember one thing based on Anthony's story... whatever your background, age, race, sex, education, "hand your dealt" or your current "success level" or "failure rate," you can always count on one thing:

Keep your faith, dream big, and always, always... TRUST YOUR HUSTLE!

Much love...and much IMPACT.

Todd Durkin, MA, CSCS
Owner, Fitness Quest 10
Lead Training Advisor, Under Armour
Author, The IMPACT Body Plan

INTRODUCTION

Every day there are about 370,000 children born in the world. On December 1, 1983, one of those children was born in Martinez, California and you have now happened upon this child's life story, my story. To think that a single child means anything special in the grand scheme of things is almost a little crazy, because I accounted for .000002% of the 370,000 children born that day, and .00000007% of the 137,000,000 children born that year making me very insignificant numerically. The truth is I was born with something great buried deep inside.

It took me many years and many, many hardships to find out that I have greatness, but when I did find out, I was able to dig it out and light a fire so hot, and so deep, that nothing of this earth is capable of extinguishing it. It then took me many more years to come to an even greater realization. There is an old quote that says, "*A life lived in service to others is the rent we should pay to live on this earth.*" The realization I came upon is that EVERYONE has something great inside; it just takes something, or someone very special to bring it out of them. No matter how big or small you may be, you should never be allowed to act small and waste the life you have been given on this earth. You are destined to do great things if YOU decide you are, and will be able to see it through to the end. Most times it is someone we happen upon in life; then again it may be the person himself. Once I discovered that everyone has this greatness inside, I took on a personal life purpose to bring it out of everyone I possibly can.

I know the questions running around your mind right now. What makes you think you are worthy of doing it? Or, what makes you think you can bring that out of someone? I believe that people who decide to take on a life purpose like mine have their own unique reasons and ways of accomplishing this. Their lives lead them along a special path that allows them to have unique experiences that others can relate to; by finding a piece of that person's story that speaks to them. My way of helping people is unique to me, and therefore the world as well. The way I will be capable of helping people will be different than the way other people like myself have been able to help. My way is special, and it is truly quite simple in its concept.

Now, if I shared it in this introduction, you may not feel the need to read the rest of this book and you may miss out on learning something life changing. For that very reason—and for the reason that I want it to hit your heart the way your brain needs it to, so it sets in thoroughly for YOU—you must read on. Keeping in mind that the root of accomplishing life success lies within your ability to trust externally, whether it be people or God, but more importantly internally. I want you to read this book about me and go on a journey of emotional heights that will make you feel like you're soaring above the clouds on a carefree sunny day with the warmth of the sun on your back and not a single worry in the world, all the way down to what it physically feels like to have the person closest to your heart stab you in the back, and then take that same knife out and use it to cut a hole in your chest, ripping your bleeding heart out with vigor, then squeezing it in front of your face with a ghastly grimace. Then have it thrown to the ground at your feet, stomping on it before lighting it on fire and burning it into ash.

The story you are about to read has been told by me many times before over the years, but NEVER like this; never with the attention to detail, or full-blow in-depth explaining of specific events. All stops will be pulled on this journey, so please strap in and enjoy the ride. I only ask one thing of you, the reader; please do not feel sorry for me. The things you are about to learn of me were experiences God meant for me, experiences I have ultimately overcome to make me the man I am today. I am capable of having the tools and life experiences necessary to write this book and help the people I was put on this earth to help. The very purpose of this book is to be able to allow my children, and my children's children, the ability to know me long after I am gone, in hopes that this story will inspire them and the world to be great! In much the same way I decided to be greater than people may have ever given me hope to be.

I thank God every day for the life experiences he gave me and more so the strength of mind and body to endure, allowing me the ability to have a unique perspective, and to be so very thankful for each and every day. Those same experiences, along with the strength he gave me, allow me to share my story in hopes of helping others. Many people have lived, or are living, lives much worse than mine. Of this I am fully aware, but they do not all have a point of perspective that I have been blessed with. Sadly, too, they often end up making poor life choices that lead them down a dark path. I hope I can prevent even one soul from doing that by sharing my story. This is just my story, so obviously to me it is very significant, just like every person's life is significant to them. Every life is significant in my eyes and EVERY person is capable of achieving so many great things in their life. The problem is that people fail to see their own light and how to shine it, or worse, how to have the enduring drive to make the light they actually KNOW they have finally shine. I personally loathe laziness & wasted talents and as you continue to read you will understand why. I just hope my story provides people a new perspective on their own lives and how to FINALLY take the necessary actionable steps to create their own success. Perspective precedes enlightenment, which is the "ah ha" moments, and without those "ah ha" moments in life we all lack the ability to grow and see the amazing things attainable in this world.

I want to provide you the motivation and inspiration to go out and make yourself great, but I also want to highlight the hidden tools I used throughout my life, usually unbeknownst to me, to do and be more than I thought I was capable of. Yes, everyone uses those same words and they all want to inspire you to greatness, but for me it's different. It's not about motivating you to do great, it's about motivating you to motivate YOURSELF. It's about digging deep inside to learn to TRUST YOUR HUSTLE.

In the following pages you will learn about me and the depths of my life that involved torture, emotional and physical abuse, love, anger, hatred, fear, amazing triumph, death, loss, heartbreak, marriage, an affair, sports success, business success, my children, and so much more. It will give you an in-depth look at what it means to climb from the deepest depths to the peak of life and happiness. You will be shown what it means to truly TRUST YOUR HUSTLE to achieve great things. Mostly I want you to see first-hand that it's not where you start that determines where you finish, it's where you finish. Having a new perspective on life doesn't change your life, working smarter AND harder from that new perspective does. THAT is true HUSTLE.

I fully realize that hearing a unique and inspiring story, or seeing a great movie, isn't enough to help someone change their life; it's the useable tools you gain from the story and apply to your own life that does. So I want to share with you my perspective, which allowed me to Trust My Hustle and be where I am today.

CHAPTER 1:

THE DASH BEGINS

For those of you who have never heard the story of *the dash*, it is a simple yet powerful story. A man is asked to give a eulogy at a friend's funeral. At the podium he asks the attendees what they think is the most important part engraved on the tombstone. After multiple incorrect answers he offers it up, "It is the dash between the day this person was born, and the day this person passed." The reason it is so important is because it represents the actual life lived by that person. It is the reason every person attended the funeral that day. It is the direct reflection of ALL the things accomplished by that person and the people affected by that person daily throughout their life. It is how their God, wife or husband, kids, parents, friends, co-workers, or anyone they may never meet will remember them for eternity. Maybe they won't even be remembered at all.

Think about all the people in this world who have left an amazing impact on the world with their dash. What makes them different than you? The truth is they are given the same amount of time each day as you are, they have just chosen to do more with it than the "average" person. Well I have a news flash for you, YOU WERE NOT CREATED TO BE AVERAGE!! So stop wasting time being average and be GREAT. The true life's question in my eyes is; how will YOUR dash be remembered? Have you thought of that yet? I have, and I want to make sure I help every person I can not only dig deep to decide what that dash is, but ACTUALLY achieve that dash. The hard part is not "wanting" to do it, but rather taking the action DAILY to do it. THAT, my friend, is the true challenge. Can you endure life's hardships to create the life that exists if you MAKE it exist?

I have spent my life enduring hardships and helping others to endure and create the life they envision by simply applying an idea that came to me only a year ago that explained to me why I have become the man I am today. My only feeling of regret in life came recently when someone asked me why I have not shared my story on a larger scale to help as many people in the world as possible. The truth is, I did not feel it was quite yet time, until recent events in my life made it clear to me that it was in fact time to push out. I awake every day with a burden on my heart that most people couldn't understand, myself included. I feel as though God made me his own personal pincushion, and for so many years I hated him for it. It wasn't until my perspective changed that I realized why I had, from a young age, met so many hardships in my life. I believe it wasn't because he wanted me to suffer, it was because he didn't want others to suffer in ways I did. He placed so many obstacles in my life, but more importantly he placed in my heart an ability to work through all of these hardships to come out stronger and more humble on the other side, and then have the strength to share my story in a unique way that helps others find triumph for themselves. We are ALL the same; we just have different experiences and ways of dealing with those experiences.

I would like to think that on December, 1983 the heavens opened up and God himself ushered me into the world, but truth be told, I was just another young black child being born to a young, poor, unwed, single white mom at a county hospital in Martinez, California with all the makings of a future criminal. Statistically, it was a long shot to think I would make it out of my teens years without being in jail or dead. This was my start. Although it seems odd, I don't look upon that day as negative because "I" was being brought into the world. I was brought home that very day and told I was a blessing to my mom. My biological father was nowhere to be found, leaving my mom alone to fend for this child—her first of four children to be born in the next three years. Before the age of 3 I do not have any memory. What I am sure of is that my mother birthed three more children in under a four-year period. My three siblings, for this story, will have their names changed for their privacy. Marsha was second born, a year behind me, Liam was third born, two years behind me, and Tillie was fourth born, 3 years behind me.

My first memory as a child was not the warmest one, and that is being stated nicely. Most children's first memory happens in their early years around age five or six and it's usually a nice warm feeling of being held, kissed, played with, or some kind of happy feeling. I wish I could say the same for myself. We stayed in a little three bedroom apartment in a complex in Concord, California, just outside our unit was a garbage dumpster. I remember the horrible smell that kicked up from the dumpster when the wind blew. My memory is so vivid of this time in my life that I can still easily remember every detail in the layout of the apartment.

I remember one very specific day where my mom Molly, who I loved so very much, called me to come outside from where I was playing alone with my toys in the living room.

I got up and scurried outside on my two little legs. As I exited the back door without a worry in the world I laid my eyes on the face of my mom crying as I approached. Molly's black hair was frizzy against her pale white skin; her eyes so full of tears I could barely see her eye color. She stood a plump 5'5" in a black T-shirt and I remember feeling uneasy and confused by the way she looked, so sad and confused. All of a sudden she leaned down and gave me a big hug and a kiss as a tear rolled down her face, touching my own. I had no idea why she was so sad as she said good-bye to me, or why she was saying good-bye at all. But the moment filled me with a fear I can still feel in my gut to this day.

When someone gripped me by the shoulder, I turned to face an unfamiliar female face, who then gently took my hand. The woman looked like she was in her mid-thirties with dark hair, and a round uninviting face. This woman gave my mom a nod and began leading me away towards a black car. I recall looking back at my mom, then at the car as the distance increased between my mom and me. I couldn't understand the look on her face; it was a look of despair and pain I had never seen come from those eyes before. The sound of Molly's muffled cries rang in my ears as I tried to make sense of this traumatizing experience. If someone had been filming me at that moment they would have witnessed one of the most confused and painful faces a tender 3-year-old child can make. A child usually does not remember things so vividly at such a young age, unless they are traumatic enough. To this day, I cannot shake the feelings of anger, disarray, confusion, sadness, and yearning I had at that very moment. When I look back on this moment I can't help but have a very sound sense of being emotionally torn between anger, and happiness because of how my life would unfold.

As I neared this ominous black car, I was finally placed in the front seat of this car I had never seen before in my life, then buckled in by the hands of a stranger. Then the door of the Ford Crown Victoria was closed. My tiny hands clawed at the door, trying to raise my little body high enough to see out of the window and see my mom, but I wasn't tall enough. Fear clouded my mind. I was oblivious to my surroundings until the silence of my racing mind was broken by the sounds of three other crying children. I turned toward the back seat where the sounds were coming from. As the driver's door opened, sunlight shone into the back seat just in time for me to see my three other siblings also strapped into their seatbelts. Behind me was Marsha, Tillie in a car seat in the middle, and Liam behind the driver. Tillie was too small to comprehend what was going on, as she was almost a newborn baby; the other two faces were like looking in the mirror and seeing the same pain and confusion. None of us had any idea what was going on and all we could do was act upon our instincts about this horrible situation and cry until the tears made it impossible to see.

I don't know how long that car ride was, but it felt like a cross-country trip. We were driving and I had no idea where or why. The oddest thing was that I don't remember a single word of comfort coming from the driver of the vehicle. As we drove for what seemed like an eternity, I don't recall a single glance from this nameless person, and it made the situation we were in feel even scarier. It seemed like days before the car came to a complete stop at a house I had never seen before. For the first time, I heard words escape the driver. "Don't move, I'll be right back." The driver turned off the car, opened her door, and then exited. As I sat there in complete and utter confusion, I could only think about wanting to be consoled by the one and only person I knew capable of doing so, my mom, but she was nowhere to be found. I searched outside the window for any sign of a place I could recognize, but my eyes were disappointed. Eventually the unfamiliar face returned and proceeded to open the rear passenger door behind me. She reached down and unbuckled my sister Marsha and motioned for her to get out, taking her by the hand. She then leaned in again and unbuckled Tillie's car seat and lifted her out of the car. Once both of the girls were removed from the vehicle she closed the door behind them, leaving only my brother Liam and I staring into each other's blank eyes.

My body started to feel physical pain as fear curled up inside of me, squeezing my insides, and it got even worse as more familiar faces were removed from my life. It was now just my brother and me, and we were still so very oblivious to what was going on. After another long break, which seemed to take years, the same face that was now growing darker in my eyes, opened the driver side door, alone. I felt a form of hatred for her. It seemed to be the cause of so much pain in my life right now, which looking back may be the reason for her cold demeanor; having experienced situations like this in the past.

The woman placed the key in the ignition and with a rumble we drove away. At that moment my heart slammed inside my chest; the feelings of loss so overwhelming. I was so scared and it all started to sink in. I was now without my mom and my sisters and I had no clue if I would ever see them again, or even why I wasn't seeing them now. The woman drove the vehicle as if she didn't even realize we were in the car. The long ride ended with an abrupt stop in front of a house I was sure I had never been to before.

When the engine was turned off, the woman turned to look at me, saying something that I can't remember. Although I cannot recall what she said, I know that the words struck me with fear; I knew it meant it was my time to leave and, after seeing the house, I wanted nothing to do with this new place. She proceeded to get out of the car then walked to the rear of the vehicle and opened Liam's door. She then leaned in and unbuckled Liam from the car and guided his hand as his little body slid out of the vehicle before the door was closed behind him. I lost sight of the two as they disappeared around the rear of the vehicle. The fear soared through my body as a feeling of panic overtook me. I was now completely alone in a car I had never been in, in front of a house I had never seen before, and in the care of a person I had never met. This feeling of internal loneliness would be a staple of my life forever, as it would be the first of many instances in my life where I would feel alone and confused, trying to figure things out without the information to do so. That feeling even follows me today at the age of 30 as I try to figure this world out; the only difference is that I have now found strength in accepting that fear, and using it to my advantage.

I remember jolting slightly at the shock of now having my door opened and having the same woman and her unfamiliar hands reaching over to unclasp my seatbelt. Her hand then grabbed my hand and I was lead out of the car onto the sidewalk. There was no one outside; not even my brother Liam. I looked frantically for a familiar face or structure, just SOMETHING to give me a sense of ease. My little heart raced as if it would beat out of my chest as I was dragged closer and closer toward a house that was brand new to my eyes. We arrived at the door and the woman knocked twice with her right hand. Now, this is where something changed. The woman then looked down to her left side where I was standing and gripped my hand a little tighter as she made eye contact with me and graciously smiled with one of the most warm and reassuring smiles I had experienced up to that point, outside of the look of my mother. For that split second, I forgot about the fear that was gnawing away at my insides because I was finally getting something that I had been yearning for this whole day, care and compassion to make me feel at ease.

The door was then opened and man and a woman with bright smiles and overall inviting and warm looking faces greeted us. For sake of the story I'll name them Bob and Sue although I do not recall their actual names. I was led through the doorway and the man and woman squatted to greet me with a warm hug before leading me into a sunken living room where I found my brother Liam playing with toys in the center of the room. I all but forgot the fear I was experiencing. The next thought in my head was simply to do what I had been doing before any of this had even begun; play with toys in the living room. I don't recall the next moments exactly, but I do however remember small segments of my time at this home. My brother and I were the only children living in this home, which seemed to be designed for children. I didn't know what that meant at the time, but looking back it must have meant that we weren't the first children to be in this predicament.

I can completely recall the entire layout of the house and the backyard as if I am walking it in my head now. Just past the sunken living room was a sliding glass door leading outside to a concrete patio filled with toys and a colorful table full of art supplies. I drew a rainbow similar to one we had seen one morning. Bob and Sue promised us that one day we would take a trip to the end of the rainbow to find the leprechaun and his pot of gold. The most memorable event in this house happened on the first night that we were there. I was sleeping on bunk beds for the first time in my life and I thought it was cool that I could be up on top and look down at my little brother below me. He was obviously too young to be able to talk, but I can't forget how cool it felt to be up that high.

That night was probably the hardest night I could re-member. I was in an unfamiliar home, with unfamiliar people, and my mom, who had been there to tuck me in every night, was nowhere to be found. Although it had been a welcoming day, taking my mind off the negative situation at hand for a brief while, it all came crashing in, as I lay there alone on a new bed. It's a scary feeling not having any sense of "base" or comfort with where you lay your head. That night I eventually fell asleep only to be awakened by a feeling of confusion, panic, and immense pain. I woke up on the floor, which means I had fallen out of the bed, and had obviously injured my right arm because the pain I felt was immeasurable. Bob and Sue came rushing into the room and embraced me, and after making sure I was O.K, they placed me back in bed and that was the end of my recollection of that night.

I can't remember how long we were at this house, but I do remember leaving. One day I was led to the front door with a bag, then outside where my body was freezing. As my eyes adjusted to the bright sun, I was eventually able to take in the surrounding details of the exterior of the house, then suddenly my eyes fixed on something I had seen before—a black Ford Crown Victoria. I had all but forgotten the fact that I wasn't home because Bob and Sue had been so nice, but seeing this familiar car, all the feelings of pain and confusion came rushing back. I was so scared at the sight of this vehicle that I couldn't move. Now, oddly enough, those feelings were short lived as a new thought crept into my head, "I'm going home." Once the thought of returning home crept into my head, I was overjoyed and couldn't get to the car fast enough. I don't recall ever saying goodbye to my brief foster parents, but I do remember thinking about the fact that we never did take our trip to the end of the rainbow.

This time the ride in the Crown Victoria would lead us back to the home I had recently left, where I resided with my mom. My feeling of yearning slowly disappeared as the car approached my house. As we pulled up I saw my sisters Tillie and Marsha outside playing, but my mom was nowhere to be seen. Getting out of the vehicle I all but sprinted back to the only place I'd known to be my home, and my brother and I greeted our sisters with hugs. As the social worker walked up I noticed a familiar face enter the picture, my mother Molly. The look on her face was not the look I expected however. It was as if she didn't really care that we were back. I ran up to hug her and she all but shrugged me off. This moment is vivid in my mind because I felt unloved and unwanted by the only person I wanted affection from.

My memory of that moment stops there and the next few years are a blur of different homes and many different interactions with my mother. That moment, in hindsight, immensely impacted my life, and for the first time I felt so very alone. Although I had siblings I didn't have the love of my mother. It was the first time in my life that the world was telling me, "You don't matter."

Putting these words down on paper forces me to re-visit emotions I have not felt in years. No child deserves to have first memories like this, but it was a critical point. That memory is the base of me, and the necessary root to my being, in ways that I have grown to understand over the years.

CHAPTER 2:

CHILD<u>R</u>EN LEFT BEHIND

If you were to read any current psychology studies on the most important developmental stages of a child, you would most likely find that the most important years are around the ages 3 to 6. In this time frame a child develops his or her emotional base, which usually comes from love and warmth from their loved ones. I was eventually placed back in foster care when I was picked up for a second time at my mom Molly's request. Sadly for me, where most children are hugged, loved, read to, played with, etc., I was experiencing the complete opposite. So many children enter the foster systems at young ages and are almost literally left behind. Some of the families they are placed with don't see them as a person, and I can personally attest to this. I am positive that for many homes I was in, I was simply a paycheck, and the less money spent on me meant more money spent on whatever else the parent wanted or needed. Essentially I was not even looked at as equal, I was just this living, breathing source of income for some people, and as long as I didn't die, all was well. Between the ages of 3 and 6 more negative experiences have been seared into my mind than any child even double my age should ever have to know.

I remember being taken to homes where I was treated horribly and every time I would go home for short stays, all I could think of is "Why am I so bad that my mom doesn't love me enough to keep me?" "What can I do to make her love me more?" "What's wrong with me?" I was taken to homes where I would be a "tester" child for families who wanted to try out a kid to see if they wanted one. One family I went to had both parents and three of their own kids. There I had my very own room, with my own TV where I watched a show on how to drive into a skid when you lost control on a wet road. This house was always clean, I was well fed and bathed, and all during the week the family bragged about the trip to Disneyland they were taking. This house was heaven to me and I was so excited that I couldn't sleep; all I dreamed about was the trip to Disneyland and being here forever. The trip day soon arrived and my heart pounded with joyous excitement at the opportunity to go with them. I had my bags packed, but as I went to get into the family car I was redirected to a black Crown Victoria. The sight of this black car might as well have been a dagger in my heart, and the chill of fear that ran through my little body is impossible to explain with words. I was again headed to another home, and another rug had been pulled from underneath me. I was simply a child to be tested to see if a family wanted a kid themselves. This sadly was one of the best memories I have during this time frame.

There were homes where I was both physically and mentally abused. One home I stayed at would only allow me to eat one small French fry from Weiner schnitzel the entire day. I remember this because there was another boy in the home with me named Scott and we used to see how slowly we could eat. At night we would sneak into the kitchen together and find any food we could and take into the room and eat it together, hiding the remains in the sides of the bed for another day. We would sneak in and grab little bites while the other would be a lookout. One day while I was inside grabbing a bite Scott failed to notify me of our foster mom approaching; I got caught. She pulled back the bed to reveal a pile of half eaten food and empty wrappers, which resulted in me being beaten. There was a feeling of sudden pain across my face and repeated hits to my little body while I writhed in pain and screamed for her to stop.

I blamed the boy for my beating, but in reality it wasn't his fault. Why would you beat a child for simply wanting to eat? Why was I such a bad kid? Why ME?

There was a house in Pittsburg, CA. where I would be forced to chase the chickens in the back yard, and if I was able to catch one, then I could eat. If not, then I would go to bed hungry. Can you imagine a 5 or 6 year- old child chasing a chicken in hopes to simply eat? I am 30 years old now and that today would be a difficult task. This screwed with my head so much at the time. I was completely out of breath and looking at their cruel faces, laughing evilly and hysterically at my misfortune by not being able to catch a chicken so I could eat that night.

The most physically and emotionally detrimental home I was ever in was located in Bay Point, CA. and I can still remember the location of the house. The vision in my head of the house standing from the curb still gives me chills. The filthy driveway with two broken down and rotting cars was to the left with a front door that faced the driveway. Inside the home felt dirty and I could not shake it. The living room was immediately to the left and to the right was a hallway that led down to the three bedrooms where as many as seven people lived. Attached to the kitchen was a sort of atrium-like glass building where food was grown, and it reeked throughout the entire house. The main parent of this home was named Doris. She had a husband and a son who was about 9 or 10 years-old while I was about 5 or 6.

Doris was a cold-hearted heavyset black woman whose very sight was terrifying. When she scowled it was fair to expect a loud vulgar sentence to escape her lips, followed, with me, by a flurry of painful closed-fist punches. Throughout my travels and between all the homes I lived in, I never feared any location quite like I feared this one. My days were spent trying to be as still and as quiet as possible in an effort not to induce a beating for something as simple as knocking over my Legos and making too loud of a noise. These Legos were the only possession I had at the time and they were my only means of entertainment, so when I was too scared to even play with them, I felt as though I was lost and all I could do was cry.

In this home I recall many painful experiences that, I now realize, should never have warranted the abuse I received. On many occasions I would be beaten in the middle of the night because I would sleep the opposite direction in my bed, simply because I feared the window above my headboard and a monster coming in to get me; which is not that uncommon for a 6 year-old in a scary, unfamiliar home. So on nights when I would not be able to sleep until they went to sleep, and I could reverse my position, I would simply lay awake holding out before the monster came for me. I would then flip myself around and hope I would wake up at the sound of footsteps so I could switch back before Doris found me. On evenings where I was not fast enough, I would wake to hard punches to my face and stomach, and the yanking of my arms to get me to flip around in the opposite direction. This would, on some occasions, startle me so much I would reactively wet the bed. On these occurrences, you can be sure that I would be physically abused much longer while the sheets were changed. I would be yanked out of bed, pushed to the ground, shoved violently and sometimes kicked, then thrown back in bed, all with tears streaming down my face from fear of not only the imaginary monsters, but the real ones that I was looking to for comfort and love. The bed wetting got so bad that I developed a long standing bed wetting problem that followed me for years, admittedly into my middle school years on occasion, but I will get to that later.

On my way to school I would walk down the road to a nearby church with my older foster brother Shawn, Doris's son, where the bus would pick us all up and take us to school. There was one very memorable morning where I was late getting to the bus stop and had to run back to the house with Shawn to ask his dad Mark to take us to school. He became filled with anger at having to get up and drive us.

In his tiny flatbed truck, with me by the door and Shawn in the middle, Mark waited for the light to turn green at the intersection. When it did, Mark forcefully hit the gas to turn left and when he did, he simultaneously leaned over to open my door, causing me to fall out into the intersection with cars right behind me. I sat there while cars whizzed by, scared for my life; all I could do was freeze up. As I looked up, I saw that Mark had parked the car and was running over to get me. I got up and ran towards him, looking for comfort from the fear I was experiencing; instead he proceeded to yell, grab my left arm, and drag me to the car. Then Mark threw me in the car and slammed the door.

When he got in, he obviously noticed blood on my face, and that angered him more for some reason. His initial reaction was to slap me and scold me for falling out of the car and making him look stupid. Then he grabbed my shirt and used the bottom of it to clean off my blood from my face. The most baffling part of the entire situation was why—why would essentially push me out of the car, and then get angry at me for falling out. I couldn't figure out what had happened or why I had been in trouble and treated that way. Emotionally I was beyond confused and it was just one of the many events of my younger years that are seared into my brain and heart.

It was nothing for me to be left alone on multiple occasions, one of which happened to be the day of the 1989 bay area earthquake. I remember feeling sudden fear as I ran outside to see all the neighbors on their lawns looking at each other in confusion. The worst part about being left alone was the massive fear of who would come home to greet me first. Oddly, the worst fears did not arise from my foster parents, but from their seemingly spiteful son who was quite possibly the worst brother a foster kid could have. Imagine being afraid of everyone in your home, but most afraid of the one closest to you in age, someone you assume should be your best playmate. Shawn tormented my life in ways that were borderline evil, and no matter what I told Doris about his actions she either did not believe me, or worse, did not care.

On many occasions I would be playing by myself quietly in my room with my Legos and Shawn would walk into the room and kick over the Lego's, then kick me. He seemed to get some sort of joy out of seeing me cry. My worst memories occurred when it was just me and him at home. He would force me to go outside with the neighborhood kids then proceed to force me to do painful and demoralizing things, apparently to show off his authority and control over me, this tiny child he could force to do things with no consequence. He gained visible pleasure in causing me pain and it literally broke my spirit at a young age.

On one occasion a group of about eight kids led me to a nearby street. To reach this street you would walk out of my house then take a left and go about three blocks down, then you would arrive at the top of a hill that led down into a curb about a block away as it dead ended at a cross street. Lucky for me on this walk the kids found a shopping cart from a nearby grocery store that was left by someone on the side of the road. At first the kids pushed the cart for fun, then Shawn had the great idea of putting me in it and pushing me around. At first I loved the idea and I was having fun. I had a feeling of joy and happiness that I hadn't felt in years as I assumed Shawn was for once playing with me as a caring brother. All of a sudden I felt the inside belly swirls of speed. As that feeling increased, ending up at the top of the next street's hill, I got that gut-dropping feeling of knowing what was to come next. My heart rate sped up when I felt myself careening down the hill. All I could hear was the boisterous evil laughs of kids enjoying the sight of my obviously fearful face while the cart went out of control and down the hill towards a busy street. I ultimately would run full speed into a curb that would launch my little body onto the hard ground of the house in front of the curb.

As I neared the street, luckily there were no cars, but seconds later I was met by a curb that did exactly what I thought it would do. The cart, with rattling wheels and a vibration I could feel in my teeth, stopped dead in its tracks against the curb and launched me out of it. I remember the sudden impact and the immediate excruciating pain that followed. Then my emotions were all over the place; feelings of pure anger, loneliness, pain, and so many more emotions. I was like a pet being tortured by people completely out of my control.

I lay there crying for what felt like forever before the group of kids eventually made their way to me where I writhed in pain. The kids, for the first time ever, showed a form of remorse that was encouraging to me as they helped brush me off to see if I was O.K. They helped me up and told me I would be O.K, then gently guided me back to the street and eventually back up the hill, as we were apparently headed back to my house. When we finally reached the top of the hill, to my dismay, my nightmare would not be over. My foster brother turned me around to face the same shopping cart that had been brought back up the hill, and then placed it in the same starting position as before.

My heart froze in fear at the thought of going back down. I can only imagine how violently I fought the kids as they grouped together, each grabbing one of my arms and legs, picking me up and forcing me back into the cart of death. The same fearful ride was repeated and ended in the same way, Me. A curb. Excruciating pain. Feelings of complete worthlessness. Sadly, this was one of the many physically demeaning events that didn't compare to the psychologically demoralizing experiences I would later be subjected to by my foster brother.

One memorable day after school I was home alone waiting for someone to come home. To my dismay Shawn arrived home first. I remember this day because he was being nice to me for once. He asked if I wanted to go outside, and I remember reluctantly agreeing to do so. When I got outside, all the neighborhood kids were there as usual, sitting on the curb in front of my house. I walked over and joined them. After a few minutes of conversation the topic of gum being stuck on the bottom of one of the kid's shoes came up, and how to get the bottom of his shoes clean. My foster brother came up with an idea that would become one of the most painful and scarring experiences of my life. His idea was for me to lick clean the bottom of his tattered muddy shoes with filth and gum stuck to them until they were clean.

I tried to get up but he managed to pin me down to the curb with the weight of his body. He then wrapped his left arm around my neck, placing my head in a full headlock, while he used his right hand to force my mouth open. I struggled with all my might, spitting while forceful breaths escaped my lips violently. The tighter he squeezed, the more I fought him while he proceeded to cut off my air supply. The boy with the gum-shoe made his way over to me and took off his shoe with the intentions of having me lick his shoes clean. I fought with all the strength my little body could produce as he rubbed the bottom of his dirty shoe up and down across my lips. I tried to get loose and stop but after a few minutes I realized I was not going to get away without giving in. I finally gave up and ended up spending what seemed like hours being forced to lick the bottom of this kids shoe with an arm around my neck, and a hand on my chin guiding the motion of my tongue. All the while I heard cackling; voices laughing hysterically at my pain, voices I had, sadly, become used to.

Once I finished with his shoe, tears were streaming down my face and again I tried to get loose, but they had no intention of letting me off the hook that easily. I spent what was probably close to literally 20 minutes being forced to lick the bottoms of all of the neighborhood kids' shoes while I cried and screamed at the top of my lungs for the tortuous pain and humiliation to stop. I can faintly remember the taste of blood and dirt on my tongue, and the thought of it turns my stomach still. I felt like a worthless soul, like I was worth nothing as a human being. No one should ever have to feel such a low in his or her life, physically or emotionally. I. Was. Nothing.

* * *

I was allowed home visits with my mother for brief periods where I would go to her home and hang out with her, essentially begging her time and time again to let me stay with her. I would clean the house to try and earn her love and show her I wasn't bad. Why should a 6 year-old be fighting for his parent's love and affection? I did not have the answer then, and I do not have the answer now. Not to mention the intense feelings of being unloved and unwanted by the very people tasked to look out for me, and provide a loving and warm environment.

To be mentally and physically abused to the extent of thinking it is normal for everyone to be treated like that as a child, is wrong. I soon developed horrible stealing and food hording habits because I had to steal and hide food to simply eat. I started wetting the bed from fear and emotional distress. I emotionally checked out because I wasn't shown love by anyone in my life. I turned cold, for obvious reasons. I was blatantly told by my world that I was worthless as a person and I was about as low as an animal you poked and prodded just to see it writhe in pain. At the same time I wasn't able to even see or know where my siblings were located, and my mother rarely ever showed up for her scheduled visits in Martinez, where I would be transported by a social worker to see her. So I would sit for hours alone.

As hard as I try, I may never be able to put into words

the totality of painful emotions experienced in my first six years of my life. Alone may be the most perfect word to explain my feelings every single day. I was alone in my personal life by not having a single solitary friend or loved one to communicate with at any given time. I was alone emotionally inside every day because I didn't know how to emotionally deal with the hurt and anguish built up inside my heart. I was alone in love because no one showed me love. I was essentially alone in every sense of the word that you can imagine, and the loneliness blackened my heart so much so I just simply stopped caring. My resentment for the world built up as I simply quit caring anymore. I learned that getting close to someone only resulted in pain.

The most important times are when a child is developing emotionally. All the things that happen affect their ability to build upon in life. Let's just say that my base was far from being solid, in fact it might as well have been built on water. Many times in my adult life I have been asked by those closest to me why I rarely cry, and the true answer is that I cried for so many days and nights as a child I think I might possibly have cried enough tears for a lifetime. I do not know if a day went by for years that I did not cry myself to sleep repeatedly. "Why me?" I asked myself this question over and over again, with no answer. Heartache, pain, and abuse became my normal. I was being forged by negative fire day in and day out. If you are wondering, like

I did for years, how I survived, you'll have to read on. The answer is not a clear one, but it does exist.

CHAPTER 3:

THE FALSE SUMMIT

If you are familiar with hiking or climbing in any way then you will understand the concept of a false summit. This is when you see what appears to be the top of the mountain and you journey towards it, giving everything you have just to reach the top. Then once you reach this summit you come to find that you're not even close, and it is usually nowhere near the top or the end of your journey. This is how the next phase of my life felt.

Have you ever been deathly afraid of something, but then, after experiencing something far worse, find that the sight of the thing that used to terrify you now only makes you feel elated? As creepy as that may sound, that was what I felt as a 6-year-old when I arrived home from school one day after school while living with Doris. I noticed an all too familiar sight that used to give me deathly chills. I saw the black Crown Victoria that was ready to pick me up and take me somewhere else. I can still feel the upwelling of happiness in my heart at that moment. But amazingly enough, I could not wait to get into that car! I knew that no place could be as horrible as this.

Getting out of the car door was a blonde-haired, middle-aged woman carrying a box of my belongings. She walked up to me and proceeded to lead me to the car before I even had a chance to enter the house. I remember that Doris never even said goodbye and, believe me, I did not care. The social worker woman opened the door of the black crown Victoria that was parked in front of the house in the exact location where I was forced to lick the neighborhood kids shoes. She placed my belongings in the back of the car, and then she opened up her own door, got in, and buckled herself up as she looked into my eyes and flashed a warm smile. She started the car and we drove off.

Here I sat in the car with a strange woman, who seemed as lost as I was, but she quickly found her bearings and we soon pulled up in front of 47 Bryan Avenue in Antioch, CA. The house was a crude, light blue affair with long, un-mowed grass, a broken fence, weeds alongside a cracked concrete driveway, and an overall appearance of dirt and disarray. After getting out of the car I was led to the front door where I was welcomed by bright, smiling, welcoming white faces. There in the doorway stood two white women and three kids. One woman was about 5'8" tall, slender build, with dark brown hair that rested on her shoulder. The other woman was about 5'6" tall, heavier set, with dark brown hair as well. Both had smiles that seemed to light up the dark doorway. I would come to find that the shorter woman was my new foster mom Grace and the taller woman was her sister, my aunt Anne.

The first room I came to I found toys. As far as I knew this was temporary so I had no interest in getting to know them. My foster moms, on the other hand, had a deep interest in me and my well-being. These people seemed different. This place felt right. Many years later I would have a conversation with my aunt Anne who described her recollection of this day in words that brings chills to my skin and tears to my eyes even now.

Anne said that I arrived a 6-year-old, 3-foot tall, skinny, dirty black boy with a head full of matted black hair that could only be described as a poorly maintained Afro. I was wearing a black girl's t-shirt that was in fact too small for me and showed my stomach. My bottoms were a pair of dirty, purple corduroy pants that barely covered the worn black cowboy boots that contained my scrunched up feet, which were too big for the boots. How could someone do this to a child? How could you claim to take care of a child but take such poor care of him? At this point of my life as an adult, I actually feel sorry for Doris and what must have gone on in her life to put her heart in such a dark place. For many years, however, anger and sorrow filled my heart because of the pain and torture she or her son put me through. Anne said her heart cried at the sight of me from sheer disgust for my condition. Her eyes welled up as she told me this story while eating dinner one night at a Mexican restaurant. That conversation will always tug at my heart...

Although that description was sad, it was not the description that especially sticks out in my memory of that day and or of the days that followed. I actually enjoyed being at this home. In my eyes this was the summit and, for a short time, I felt comfortable. I would come to find out this home on Bryan Ave. was a far cry from normal, and although I felt better here, time would soon prove to me that I had in fact reached my false summit. I now was in a family with an older brother by two years, two younger sisters, and foster parents. My older brother Miles at the time was a very inviting kid, so far opposite from my previous foster brother. Although everyone in my new home was white, he happened to be half Mexican as my new foster mom had birthed him at the age of 14 with a man no longer in any of their lives.

My brother went on to have his ups and downs, but today he is a man I look up to, and there are few men in this world I can say that about. My two younger sisters Sally and Bonnie were what you would expect typical sisters to be, annoying most of the time. My relationship with them over the years has had its ups and downs, of the downs have resulting in words being spoken that would break a normal person. All in all I love my sisters, and they could not be any more "mine" if we were related by blood. My foster mom, Grace, was and is an amazing person with a patient heart. She has never had it easy but always did her best to love and provide for us kids over the years. She took in a kid who you will find to be more than a headache.

My first step foster father Bill, who is the father of my sisters, is someone I don't like to think about because of the type of man he was to me when I was a child. Although he is forgiven, his actions are not forgotten. He stood about 6 feet tall with a dirty blonde mullet, a dingy look, and a deep raspy voice that still makes me cringe when I think about it.

We lived in a house so unsanitary that looking back on it my stomach still turns in disgust. There were so many cockroaches in the garage that when you opened the door you could literally see the ground go from black to grey concrete. The garage was so full of random garbage that it was completely off limits, and deemed a lost cause to even enter. The kitchen was filthy, with a dark caked-on film of dirt on the white linoleum floor, a sink full of dishes that let off a putrid smell, counters lined with garbage and old food, and the spilling over with food so moldy that even the countless mice who roamed the house wouldn't touch it. Our rooms were cluttered with dirty clothes and rotten food plates strewn about. The living room and hallways were lined with trash bags full of clothes or actual garbage. The clothes bags were where I would pull out damp wrinkled clothes for school on most days, clothes which resulted in my being picked on by school-mates because of my horrid appearance. Our backyard was tetanus waiting to happen. Mud and broken toys lined the entire yard, and our patio area was so dirty that calling it filthy would be a compliment. Let's just say this home was a true description of a "white trash household."

What I didn't know at the time was that I had been placed into a family that was far from perfect. My foster father Bill was an abusive alcoholic. Bill was a bulky 6 foot, dirty blonde haired, overweight white man with a belly that hung over the belt buckle on his stained blue jeans. He reeked of body odor and beer at all times of the day. He was mentally and physically abusive and, on multiple occasions he would bludgeoned me during his rampages. On one occasion I was thrown across my bedroom, head first, landing onto my wooden L-shaped bunk bed, which resulted in a blow that caused my head to bleed profusely.

I am not sure if I ever told any of the social workers about this because, sadly, I had become accustomed to this kind of behavior and by now believed it was normal.

I have a vivid memory of the last time Bill was in the home. It was a normal hectic evening at our household with the customary yelling and arguing, but on this night Bill and Grace had gotten into a bigger argument than usual in the kitchen, and we kids were watching from the doorway. She yelled at him for something he had done wrong which resulted in him bellowing vile words at the top of his lungs—words that I refuse to use even to this day. When he forcefully pushed her back and she slipped on a banana with her left foot, she slipped into a kneeling position, with her left knee on the ground. Bill then cocked his right arm back, made a fist, and brought it across the left side of Grace's face with enough force to drive her body and shoulder into the stove on her right. When she recovered enough to speak, Grace yelled at him to leave and never to come back. In some way or other he must have listened to her because that was the last we ever saw of Bill in our home.

Over the years I was most definitely not the easiest child to deal with. I was in a dysfunctional family where I woke up every single day knowing in my gut that a black car could arrive at any moment and pull me up by my roots to someplace new. Because of this fear I was unruly and just didn't care. I honestly tried so hard to be bad at times because I figured that if I was bad enough they would just hurry up with the inevitable and send me along to the next home. Between the ages of 6 to14 I lived in that void because I was not yet adopted. But when I was 14, Grace married a man named Mike who at first wasn't accepted very well by us kids. Although this young man entered our family at the age of only 20, he accepted each one of us four kids as his own. Now, although he was accepting of us, he was still a 20-year-old who didn't have many parenting skills, so we had our fair share of bad run-ins with him. It took Mike many years to gain acceptance from us kids. But to me now, he is a real world superman for what he did, and has done, for our family over the years. If any man in this world is my father, it is this man, and I am very proud to call Mike my father. That fatherless, eight-year void between the ages of 6 and 14 was the hardest time in my, life without a doubt. That is it was the hardest time until I reached the age of 28, but we'll get to that later.

What made the void so difficult was the internal unrest that occupied my soul at every waking moment. And for good reason. I was the only black person in an all-white family that wasn't even my own; so feeling disconnected would be an understatement. My home life was so unsettling that I don't recall ever being comfortable. At school I was teased every single day because in 1989 in Antioch, diversity wasn't the norm. I was called a nigger almost every day. In class I would act out every single day. Let me repeat that to make sure you understood: every single day. In the second grade I was given the ability to earn a full-size candy bar every day if I did not get in trouble even once. This lasted until fifth grade, and then I was unable to earn a single candy bar for four years.

I wasn't even allowed to go to 6th grade camp for fear I wouldn't be able to handle the woods. So I went to school alone that week, and it only got worse when everyone returned and I had to hear all about their stories of fun that I was unable to participate in. Not to mention that every single day of my life I would go home with a racing heart wondering if there was going to be a black crown Victoria waiting to take me away again.

I was actually an incredibly smart student, but my problem, in hindsight, is that my home life was so off kilter that I would release in school by attracting attention to myself and bothering other students. I actually tested for "Gate", which is a program for gifted children, when I was in the second grade because I was seen to be a gifted student by my teachers. I was, in fact, only allowed to be at kindergarten for an hour because of my poor behavior. I can remember every teacher from the first through fifth grade yelling at me at the top of their lungs, so close to my face that I could feel the heat of their breath on my forehead. Honestly, I don't blame them.

I stole anything I could get my hands on because I had developed a habit of hoarding due to being starved at previous homes. I got into fistfights with kids on the playground almost daily. I was the stinky kid in class as well, and it took physical force to make me take baths at home. I was quite possibly the worst kid you could probably imagine, and I truly feel sorry for some of my classmates and teachers back then, but I was always in a constant struggle for acceptance. I was internally a child lacking any self-worth because the person I wanted so much to love me, placed me in hell on earth, in my eyes. I hated being at school 90% of the time, and my home life wasn't always rainbows and smiles.

At home I lived in a constant state of fear and disconnect because I had already built up walls that kept everyone at a distance. In foster care you don't fully know why you are where you are, and my biological mom Molly succeeded in making it so much worse for me on every level imaginable. Molly was allowed visitation in the city of Martinez but, due to her lack of appearances at the visits, the home visits went to twice a week visits at the social services offices. Soon they were once a week, then once every other week, to once a month, and finally, once every few months, and so on, until I didn't see her for months. What hurt the most was watching my other half siblings, who had the same dad, visit with him every time because he cared enough to go see them.

Don't think I didn't hear from my mother though. She managed to call me every time she missed our visit and give me a story so grand I thought she was the coolest person in the world. The stories ranged from her owning a massive company to being a registered genius through NASA. She was able to abuse me mentally and emotionally, knowing she could play with my mind and say words to deter my anger at her absences at visitations.

No matter what the story included, it seemed to end the same way. I was instructed to secretly pack a bag and wait by the window at 8 p.m. that night and she would come and get me, and we would be a family again. Recalling this very string of memories makes me want to stop writing at this moment because of the emotional pain that arises deep inside. Imagine a child between the ages of 6 and14, year after year sitting fully dressed with a bag of clothes and an enormous upwelling of hope and happiness while waiting and staring listlessly out onto an empty street. I would have my jacket buttoned up and my little hand grasping a bag packed with care, ready for my final trip home. As I saw the surrounding houses illuminate from the headlights of every passing car, my heart would flutter in anticipation of it stopping and my mom's face emerging from the car door. It. Never. Happened. I would spend the next hours a broken crying wreck as I gathered my heart pieces back up just enough to curl into a ball in my lonely cold bed, and think about the ensuing day that brought more name calling and lack of belonging.

The worst part was the bed-wetting problem that I mentioned earlier, which seemed to occur only after I had spoken to my mom when she promised to pick me up. I would sadly go to school sometimes without even cleaning myself, or the sheets. The internal suffering I felt made me feel worthless and in zero control of my emotions, or my life. I felt like I was nothing to anyone and I remember crying out loud on multiple occasions asking God, why me? Why was I suffering when I had done no wrong to deserve this? Eventually I came to realize I just wasn't worthy of a good life, and for some reason, I didn't deserve it.

* * *

I continued along this path for many years of my life and, sadly, there wasn't a year of my life that passed without some sort of unique experience that ensued. During this time of my life we lived in two houses, one of which we lived in until I was the age of 12. The first house, as previously described, was run down but it provided a wealth of special memories. We didn't have money so although this house was incredibly dirty, I do remember some pretty fun times, doing things that were out of the norm to say the least. At one point my older foster brother broke the legs off a rusty, partially white painted pair of mesh patio chairs. We tied the seat and seat backs to each other to form a square then tied them to the top of the patio overhang to make a basketball hoop with no backboard, which oddly was a blast to play on. My foster dad put together a swing set in the back yard the way most men do; halfway. We had a field day with this thing. During rainy days we would get our dirtiest clothes and shoes on and take our bikes around this white and green metal structure like it was a BMX raceway, flinging mud on everything and having an absolute blast laughing and yelling the whole time.

Once we had the bright idea of tying up one of our B.M.X. bikes by the seat and the handle bars about two feet off the ground, then took turns riding it like we were E.T., hovering over the city streets below. When we weren't outside we were inside taking apart all sorts of electronics to make fans by playing with the disassembled motors. We would attach a piece of tape to the tips of tiny electrical motors from our tape decks and hook up a battery to see them spin. We took perfectly good pieces of electronics and tore them apart to engineer other ones just for the heck of it, and our mom would be beyond angry when we did it. It was just something to pass the time, and it was in fact great bonding time with my older brother.

Since we had a decent-sized backyard and it was so

filled with random things, we managed to get very creative. One time we took the siding off of one of those old 12' plastic swimming pools then cut it to make one long strip. Then we laced up our roller skates and ran through the dirt like clomping dinosaurs until we designed the jump of death where you try to transition from running with skates to rolling out of control with skates on a two foot thick plastic strip laid on top of clumps of dirt. The front yard had weeds so high you could literally hide in it, much like a corn field; working to keep from stepping on the garbage that lined the ground.

The neighbors might as well have been on a reality show because we could watch them for hours. They had a beautiful old-school red car that the guy, a five-foot ten man who dressed like a bum from the fifties, drove. The only thing more attention grabbing than the car was the decibels at which the neighbor couple could fight, and they would go at it for hours. The lady was older and had skin that looked like a wrinkled up paper bag hidden underneath a mat of blonde hair. Her lined faced told the tale of years of drugs, and her actual body movements solidified it. One fight ended in the car getting smashed up by her hammer, and that happened to be the last we saw of her. Soon after they moved out, we kids got a chance to go into the house. You could tell the kind of people they were by the tell-tale signs that went from the literal writings on the wall, to the putrid smells and apparent devil worshipping marks carved into the paint.

If that wasn't enough excitement, we took countless camping trips where I would run along the beaches during the day or have a blast catching frogs at night and just being free. So although this wasn't anyone's ideal place to reside, we made the most out of it. Outside of the bad times, we did manage to have some good times. Besides all that, we would visit our mom's dad, Grandpa Frank, because he was such a blast. He was the most loving, caring man you would ever meet. No favor was too small to ask of him, and it never failed that you would light up inside at the sight of high pearly whites when they broke out past his lips in an ear to ear smile. He was over six-foot tall, and an Italian man with a balding head and a bushy mustache that shook when he bellowed out with laughter, kind of like a big bellied Mario. He would eventually move to Idaho and we couldn't wait for the days when he would drive down and pick us up to go visit him where he had tons of land to wander around in and horses to ride. He happened to also be the Christian figurehead of our family who provided the rock of emotional security to us when we needed it. He was a great man in my eyes. We honestly didn't have a shortage of things to get into at his home to keep us busy having fun.

Over the years I managed to make the most of the situations at school as best I could. Elementary school was a very adventurous grouping of years that played out many memorable experiences. I got into so many fights I can't remember them all, but I do remember the last one. I fought an older "tougher" kid because he wouldn't give me the basketball court I had gotten first. After two flurries of kicks and punches I left his face red and his pride hurting which earned me enough cred to not have to fight anymore. This skill came from karate classes that seemed to be the only thing Molly would let me do, because she was afraid I would get hurt playing football. Karate ended up being a good resource for my life. My grandpa Tom happened to own the school, and he was a former marine who didn't fail at give me structure and balance when under his guidance.

I kept my body in shape by riding my bike to and from karate and always being consistent like he taught me. These skills have helped me later in life, but at the time they obviously weren't being used for good. As I said earlier, I was even banned from going to my sixth grade camp because I was deemed a sort of a flight risk, so they didn't want to take the chance.

Over the years some amazing things happened at school. I met my best friend(s) for life. I have four friends that I have known since I was in the fourth grade and we are still very close, one happens to be my absolute best friend in the world, a white police officer of all things named Cliff. Over the years we have had our times of closeness and great distance, but no matter what's going on in life we will always be there for each other. Back in the early years I spent almost every weekend at my best friend Cliff's house, and we got into more trouble than any kid should because he also wasn't having the best upbringing.

As a kid I was a huge fan of Randy Moss. I would open up into a full sprint and head down the street ready to catch the long ball that Cliff prided himself on throwing, but that was about the only good thing we did. We would tie a fishing line across the street from one pole to another on the opposite side of the street at night. Then we would then wait for cars to drive by and break the string with their bumpers. One time the neighbor kids set it up while I was inside going to the bathroom. As soon as I came out I saw someone standing outside of their car and when they saw me, they ran up to me as if I had done it. They ushered me to the door to find my parents but I didn't live there. After the person drove off everyone came from behind the bushes where they had been hiding and enjoying every moment of my altercation, and scolding, from the angry stranger

One night 5 of us went for a walk on nearby trails to the store about a mile or so away. It was in the winter in

California so it was not cold, but it was pretty wet and muddy. We had this grand idea to go to the fence on the side of the trail that was up a 20 foot hill from the main street so we could make mud balls. I'm sure you can imagine what happened next. We proceeded to make six-inch round packed balls of mud and have target practice with passing cars going about 45+ miles per hour. We had to have thrown about 100 balls between us all and I cannot figure out how the cops weren't called. Cars would whizz by and "BANG" you could hear the smack of the ball on their windshield. They slammed on the brakes and swerved before continuing on. The worst was when the light would turn red. I vividly remember a Chinese food delivery van at a red light that we pelted so hard it sounded like a bomb and the side of the white van that we turned brown. That night, while walking home, we decided to take the main road where one of the kids threw a rock at a passing car, without us knowing it. The car slammed on its brakes and out came a man with a gun. We were out of there! We sprinted to a nearby fence and jumped it as fast as we could, jetting home without breaking stride. We hadn't noticed until we got home that one of our group was missing; the youngest. In fact he had beaten us home, but not by outrunning us. The driver happened to be an off duty police officer and he escorted the 10 year-old home and greeted us all with a scowl, and a stern scolding, that was later followed up with the same by the adults at home.

One of the funniest and most memorable parts of hanging at Cliff's house was a strange lady who would periodically sprint down the main road with her arms full of bags. I happen to be a former NFL player and I can tell you with full honesty that the speed at which she ran, combined with the weight of the bags and the distance she traveled at that consistent pace, could not be matched by me in even my best shape. This lady was the funniest thing we had ever seen because she ran as if her life depended on it. In all the years this happened, we honestly thought she had stolen the bags and we fully expected to see police cars flying down the street, but they never came. She didn't stop and she never spoke when we called out to her. She never slowed down; never broke her full speed stride, and we never knew where she was coming from or where she was going. To this day we think back to her with so many unanswered questions, but all we seem to accomplish is bringing up the same hearty laugh at the sight of this lady. Imagine a 5'6" white woman with dark brown, shoulder-length hair, wearing a white tank top and blue jean shorts sporting a look of pure determination while sprinting with her arms loaded with yellow grocery bags so heavy that she couldn't bend her elbows. No words were ever spoken, and she was topping for nothing short of being tackled to the ground, we know because one time we decided to follow her on our bikes and the ride ended up being too far for us to want to continue on. As far as we know, she might still be running like Forrest Gump right now.

* * *

Growing up my friends and I did things other kids did; rollerblading, bike riding, and learning every inch of our hometown of Antioch. Long days were spent coasting the street as free as birds from sun up to sun down. We would meet at someone's house and then choose a point as far away as possible and just go there. We had no destination pre-determined and that made it all the more fun. We stopped by other friends' houses, grab food, harassed people, and one night during Halloween we saddled up on our bikes and made a trip to the grocery store for some eggs that did not find their way to anyone's belly that night. Some of the fondest memories of my childhood took place with these guys over the years. The only drawback during this time was that at my house in order to be able to go anywhere I had to my chores. Yes, back then kids had chores kiddos. If you recall my house wasn't the cleanest, so chores were almost a jail sentence. Although we kids were supposed to have equal shares, I ended up doing more than my fair share because 1) I actually obeyed my parents, and 2) I would have to do my siblings chores sometimes if I wanted to go out.

In the 4th grade I actually won the school spelling bee beating out even the 6th graders and moving on to the county spelling bee where my nerves got a hold of me and I spelled the word tough, "TUFF." I eliminated myself in the first round. In the sixth grade my best friend Cliff and I ran for red track president, and won, which meant we represented the entire k-6 classes of our school on the "red" reading track in each grade; "red" was one of the four colors associated with the classes at each grade level, and boy, was that a bad idea for them. I don't think we ever even made a president's meeting, but we sure had a good campaign, and it was actually my very first speaking opportunity. I addressed the entire school reading from a crumpled white flashcard. We had a blast on the playground also as I happened to be one of the best athletes out there. I loved running on the grass during recess, but I hated being in class and it showed. I used to bug everyone around me and I can't honestly fathom how my teachers were able to put up with me. I sincerely thank every teacher for putting up with my antics and not strangling me.

I took fart spray to school and sprayed it on other kids when they weren't looking, I would throw paper balls across the room just to see if I could get away with it, and bring in electronic toys I would steal from stores when I was out with my parents. I remember one time that I was flicking an eraser at a girl student who sat across from me. My teacher said that if I did it one more time she was going to take it away from me. I was seated with my back to the teacher and when she finally put her head down to go back to work I acted as though I was going to flick it again and the girl across from me let out a whimper that resulted in my teacher shooting up from her desk and making her way towards me. When she asked me to hand over the eraser I told her I hadn't flicked it again so she had no reason to take it from me. The teacher, hovering over me, reached out to take the eraser and I balled up my little hand so tight she was unable to find a way to remove it from my death grip. I could see the frustration on the teacher's face and it somehow gave me a kick, before she kicked me out and sent me to the principal's office. I looked up at my teacher with a grimace on my face that probably looked like the Grinch, while she fought in utter frustration to get me to simply give her something that was unnecessarily being protected. It was horrible on my part, but at the time it was a blast, and I think it was all just for attention.

On another occasion our computer teacher, who was an elderly woman who had no patience, happened to see me bouncing a little green ball that I had brought from home. She told me to throw it in the garbage, to which I simply responded, "It's not garbage." You could almost see the anger bubbling from the top of her head. She quickly got up and made her way to my chair as, trying to pull the ball from my grip to no avail, which sent me on another of so many trips to the office. In retaliation I managed to steal one of the mouse balls from the old school green computers we had that happened to play Oregon Trail. When we all came to class the next time, the teacher had obviously noticed one of the balls missing. She immediately accused me but I denied it up and down. She threatened that if it wasn't returned there would be no more computer class for our classroom. Everyone blamed me and I stood strong in my denial even though I knew it was I. I even lied to my best friends about taking it. It wasn't until a couple of years ago that I finally admitted to being the one to take it to my friends, and we had a good laugh, even though it sucked at the time, resulting in my class being banned from the computer class for the rest of the year. If the picture of the type of student I was isn't clear by now, then I am unsure how better to do it justice. I. Was. Bad.

* * *

Something in me changed around the age of 12, making me a little calmer—we moved to a new home in a different part of Antioch. My mom Grace had become pregnant with my new step foster father Mike's baby girl. This was soon to be my third younger sister Rachel, and they didn't want her to be born into the old dirty house we had all spent so many years in. That would turn out to be a great decision that, over the years, led to my sister growing up into ab admirable young woman with a humongous heart and a maturity twice her age. She doesn't know it yet but she is going to do great things in her life.

A couple years later they would have their last child, my youngest brother Mike Jr. He's definitely a unique guy, but I love him to death. We are complete opposites, me being a black athlete, and him a heavy set white kid who loves dead head music and considers growling to be a singing skill.

To digress a moment, for reasons I don't quite understand, the move we made when mom was pregnant with Rachel somehow cleared my head. For the first time, I lived in a nicer house. The house was in a neighborhood of beautiful, clean homes that actually had grass in the front yards. The house was painted a cream color with soft royal blue accents and a huge backyard that had a pool, a swing set, a club house, and a nice patio area to lounge around in.

When I got to the 7th grade I cut off my disgusting afro, I stopped wearing stinky clothes, and I actually started washing and ironing my own clothes every day. I also took care of my shoes so I wouldn't have to go to school with shoes so worn that I actually laced up the holes with paper clips. I now wanted to be proud of the way I looked. Looking back, it was my first year of middle school and I think I have an idea of what it was that changed my mind. Girls. I wanted to be looked at like a "someone" for the first time, not just that stinky kid anymore. I was still a pain as a student, but I actually tried to stay out of trouble in middle school and, although I still spent my fair share of time in the office, I managed to become a better student academically.

My home life got a little better because I think my whole family was feeling more comfortable with our living situation. My dad got a job as a pipefitter and was making good money in his profession, and my mom was going to school to be a nurse. This finally felt like a normal life for once. We still didn't have much money and I remember hating being driven to school in our old poop brown Chevrolet caprice that made this embarrassing "tink, tink" noise every time you revved the engine; but hey it was what we were working with at the time. It was about this time that I began realizing that if I was going to get anything in life, I would have to do it myself. My friends had nice things like bikes, TV's, game systems, rollerblades, and other things. Since my parents didn't have the money to buy these things, I had to make the money myself. I assumed that it was possible if I worked hard enough, although I honestly didn't know. I didn't have a track record of success in anything, but I needed to start somewhere. I knew I couldn't ask anyone for money, so I figured out the money situation on my own.

My first job was raking leaves; yes raking leaves. I would go house to house asking if they would like me to rake their leaves for $5. I got lots of no's and the occasional yes, not to mention the few stick ups who would let me do the job and then not pay me, but I believe karma is a nasty foe. After a year of that I had a grand idea to follow in my brothers footsteps who years before had a paper route that I had helped him with. I joined the ranks and became a paperboy delivering newspapers every day for three years, after school during the weekdays, and mornings on the weekends. I only missed three days in three years. This taught me so much at a young age about responsibility and achieving success if you worked hard enough. I even had to deal with a customer who forced me to re-deliver his paper in the middle of opening gifts on Christmas Day. But it all turned out positively for me, because I was able to buy my first bike, which my parents gave to me at my birthday party as if they had bought it. I also bought my own roller blades, a TV, a stereo, and basically anything I wanted since it was my earnings. I was slowly learning life lessons at the age of thirteen that have continued to guide me to this very day. I couldn't have imagined back then the heights I would reach using the principles of hard work, accountability, and persistence that I developed as a paperboy.

Although things were finally feeling solid for me, I was still haunted by one thing. Every single day of my life for every one of those eight years I lived with the dread of the possibility of seeing that black Crown Victoria parked outside my house. It is probably the equivalent to checking under your bed every single night for monsters, but this one I knew was real. I deathly feared seeing it again. As the saying goes, "The devil you know is better than the devil you don't." The sickest part is that the better it got at home, the scarier it got knowing that it could all be kicked out from underneath me any day and I had no control over it. I had the ultimate feeling of a lack of solidarity and control in my life that grew worse as life grew better. It's almost as if I wished for it not to get better for fear of one day losing it all. It's a horrible feeling to endure year after year at that age.

At the age of fourteen something amazing happened that made me capable of being adopted. Just writing that brings back the feeling of positive chills running from my feet to the tip of my head. The simple possibility of knowing exactly where I would lay my head every night brought me elation. You see for eight years I was at the helm of two sets of rules in one household, which tormented me. My biological mom Molly never wanted to see me but she always wanted to tear apart the happiness I felt with my new family. She, at some point, would blame my new family for me being in foster care in the first place, although I knew the real reason— Molly had called Child Protective Services one day to say she couldn't take care of the kids anymore and we needed to be picked up. This was an opportunity for me to do something that I had dreamed about for years of my life; play football, because she would never give permission for me to play. All of my friends played and boasted about how fun it was, and I would dominate them at recess, wanting so badly to test my metal. Who knew I would go on to play in the NFL?

So one fateful day I got up, dressed up nicely, and drove with my family to the courthouse in Martinez to meet my social worker. He was a short, hunched old man with a flowing white beard that connected to nothing on the top of his head and wore a blue pinstriped suit. While with my foster parents and my social worker, I remember the awkward feeling that came over the group when my biological mom walked through the tall wooden doors of the courthouse, letting in the blinding light from outside. Molly wore a pair of tight, light blue 80's high-waisted jeans that hugged her overweight hips, held up by a black belt that could be seen when her white turtle neck sweater lifted up to show it. She had her dark brown curly hair tied back in a ponytail to show her pale white face with the brightest red lipstick. When she opened her mouth and smiled, exposing yellowing teeth, she welcomed me with outstretched arms. I didn't know what to do because I knew why I was there.

I was told earlier that I would have to take the stand and deliver the news to my mom that I no longer wanted her to be my mother or to be a part of my life anymore. At fourteen years old, it was a feat that I didn't know I had the courage to perform. We would soon find out as we were called to the docket. The judge, a tall white man in a long black robe entered the courtroom, smiled warmly and invited me to his chambers. Once in his chambers, he stated what I was doing there, what he would ask me, and how I should respond based on my feelings. He left the room and told me someone would be in to get me shortly. Before I knew it I was walking out of his chambers and heading straight to the witness stand.

As I approached the stand I could see my mom sitting alone almost directly in front of me, looking into my soul with a deep piercing gaze. To the right of me was my soon to be adoptive family that I had grown to know so deeply and love. Here was a white woman who endured literally a hellish black child and still was fighting to make me her own child, accompanied by a white man who was barely old enough to drink alcohol. Love for someone is hard to prove, but at that moment I saw proof of their love for me as their child. The judge started his questioning and led me straight to the question that still rings in my ears as if he just asked it this very moment. "Anthony, do you want this woman to be your mom?" How do you answer that question with the eyes of the first person you ever truly loved in your life looking into your soul, knowing that your answer was going to push this person out of your life?

With all I had inside of me I mustered the strength to answer, "No, I don't want her to be my mom anymore." She responded with, "He's only saying that to be able to play football. I'll let you play if that's what you want." I could see the hurt and pain in her face and I could hear it in her voice, and I immediately felt a wave of sorrow fill my heart. I went back into the judge's office and that was the last I would ever see of my mother's face in person, but not the last time I would hear her voice. My mother's rights were severed that day and a weight had literally been lifted off my chest and my life. For the first time in the fourteen years of my young life, I knew where I was going to be sleeping every night. Now for some people that may seem stupid or random, but for me it brought jubilation and a feeling I had been searching for all my life, solidarity. I. Was. Free.

I had no more qualms about whether or not I could go on trips, no more endless nights being told to wait by windows, no more infinite days coming home wondering if I would see a black car parked and packed with my belongings ready to take me away, no more missed visitations, no more double standards in one household, and the list could go on forever. For the first time in my life I didn't have such a huge worry to live with. I was internally a different, calmer person.

The next step was to change my name. I was originally named Anthony Antonio Alonzo Trucks, and now after being adopted by the Hart family I changed my name to what it currently is, "Anthony Hart Trucks," and I couldn't be more proud of my name. I knew who my mom and dad were. I had no idea who my real father was because my biological mom told me years earlier that he left her when she got pregnant, but I now had a father. I had no hopes of ever finding my biological dad who was obviously a black man, but the name on my birth certificate ended in O'Byrne, which is Irish, and this black guy probably isn't a rare black Irishman. Truth be told, I didn't care who he was and I had no desire of finding him, mostly because I would probably never even know his real name, but also because I had my dad now and I was happy with him.

* * *

Next came the first of many pivotal points in my life that started the journey for me being the man I am today. I was finally able to play football, and for most that is a simple thing, but for me it was very different and unique. The first thing I had to do was quit karate only two levels

away from a black belt that I had invested four years of my
life into. Since we didn't have much money, I had to pay
for my first year of football with my paper route money,
and I remember us not being able to even afford a pair of
cleats that fit me. I bought a pair of black and white Nike
Shark cleats that were at least two sizes too big. I rolled
up 1" thick flat sections of toilet paper and wrapped them
in scotch tape before cutting them to fit the shape of my
toes, then inserted them into the tip of my cleats to fill the
empty space inside. My mom found a local football team
that had literally just came into existence, and we were the
flagship year. So there were no cuts and Grace liked that
because she thought I wouldn't' make a team if I had to try
out and possible get cut for not being very good. We signed
up and I was now part of the Antioch Junior Wolverines.
Here is the kicker, my mom Grace was right, I sucked horribly my first year. All I could do was manage to throw the
football but I couldn't catch my own breath, let alone a
ball. With those huge shoulder pads and that big helmet I
could barely see. In games all I managed to do was tackle,
and boy was I good at that, a skill that would pay off in
time. I fell in love.

 Now you see, at this point in my life I had been shown
multiple times throughout the years that I was a nothing,
that I was lower than an animal to some people, I had zero
control of my life, that I essentially had no control of any-

thing, and I wasn't anything to the world. I felt miniscule to my peers as a human being and it made me feel chained to a sentence of a life of worthlessness. The thought of what I am about to tell you STILL sends waves of pride and happiness through my body as my skin tightens and I get goose bumps while striking these keys. For the absolute first time in fourteen years of my life "I" was in control of something. I felt like a person who mattered. When I laced up my oversized cleats, tightened the straps on my shoulder pads, buckled my belt after pulling up my pants, and snapping the clasps on my helmet before putting my shock doctor mouthpiece in my mouth, I felt in control. I could run as fast as I wanted and it was praised. I could hit someone as hard as my little body could hit and it was applauded. I could yell in triumph when I made a tackle and my team gave me high fives. I had an outlet. More than anything else, I mattered. I owned the control over these moments and NO ONE could take that away from me. There was no more fear of a black car coming to pick me up. No fear of large man or woman coming to put their hands on me. No more fear of not knowing when I would get to eat. No child holding me down forcing me to lick kids' shoes. No one telling me to be quiet, calm down, and sit. No one was in my head out on that field but me, and I controlled what happened at every single moment. For this reason, football was, and always will be, my first true love. Football gave me more in a single game than I could have asked for from any other part of life. It gave me life, a purpose, meaning, acceptance, and consistency. From the work ethic I learned in simply doing what I had to do to be able to play, to the life lessons I learned while on the field, to the priceless feeling of hope, acceptance, and belonging my heart had yearned for my entire life. All I knew is that I NEVER wanted to let that feeling go and I was going to fight to keep football in my life, for the rest of my life.

At the age of fourteen I made a decision that was very unique and that has carried me to where I am today. Now I, like everyone in life, have definitely had my pit falls, which you'll learn about as I go on, but one singular decision changed the entire course of my life. I keenly noticed one thing about the game of football and the players involved. I noticed that although I came from a completely different upbringing than my teammates, on the field, we were EQUAL. It didn't matter how much money you had, what clothes you wore, what jobs your parents had, how cool you were in school, or anything else. All that mattered was once we suited up to play, I could beat you and THAT is all that mattered. The decision I made was to look at life the same way I looked at football. It didn't matter what you had, where you came from, of who you thought you were. It didn't matter at all where you started. It ONLY mattered where you finished. I made it my life's mission to be GREATER than what the cold world had been telling me I was meant to be. The world's actions told me I was meant to be a loser, a thief, a criminal, or even worse. Based on my upbringing it would not be surprising to hear that I was dead or in jail for some hellacious criminal activity, and sadly the world would accept that as a good enough answer to why I did what I did.

FORGET THAT! I wanted to be great in terms of what greatness meant to the kids given the silver spoon. I didn't just want to be great in "comparison" to what I came from. Great in comparison to my past would be having a good job, not being a criminal, being a present father, having a solid relation with someone, and just not being a drain on society. That, in my mind, was NEVER going to be good enough. I wanted to be great in terms of the WORLD'S view of great. To be a positive light for society, to break the statistical mold of what kids like me grow up to be. I aspired to look at the world not in terms of what I didn't have to achieve my goals, but what I did have to achieve them. If I lacked in any area, I made up for it with the tools I had learned through life, pushing ahead full bore until I attained what I wanted, because THAT is what great required out of me. That is what GREAT was in this world. Mediocre is for losers and moderation is for cowards. Great was my goal, and although I didn't know what it was at the time, I knew that when I saw it I would recognize it, and I would never stop until it was mine in football and in life. This was my defining moment.

CHAPTER 4:

DEFINING MOMENT<u>S</u>

This was now a new beginning for me in life and I was going to take full advantage of it. I truly believe life is full of defining moments that alter the course of your history. Sadly, you usually don't notice them until they have passed. For me the defining moment of my life took place at the age of fourteen as I have said. As the years progressed, like all teenagers, I had my pitfalls and stupid mistakes, but they made me the man I am today. It was after the moment that I decided to be great that the world opened up to me in different ways. Some good, and some bad, but nonetheless it opened up.

My first year of football was a unique thing to me because I got to experience team sports for the first time, as well as make new friends outside of school. This is also middle school and the time when you start to like girls and go through that awkward stage of puberty that us young men all love so much. I actually got my first crush on a girl and took her to the movies. My friend Sherry and her mom, picked up me and this other girl, Ella, to go to the movies. I wore blue jeans, a white T-shirt, and one of those flannel jackets with the thick black lining and a green exterior. I was so nervous that I sweat too much and I was afraid to take it off. What no one knew was that I had ridden my bike down to the 7-11 earlier that day and grabbed a red fake rose in a plastic cellophane wrap and I intended to give it to this Ella as soon as she got in the car. The problem was that I was too nervous. When she got into the car I slipped the rose into my left jacket arm as she sat on my right and I tried my best not to bend my arm to crush it or make any noise. We rode all the way to the movie theater and I couldn't work up the nerve to give it to her. Then I tried at the movies and was again unsuccessful. Then on the way home I tried once more to muster up the ability to pull it out and present it to her. Let's just say this is the first time anyone even knew I had a rose up my sleeve for those four hours. Talk about a crash and burn first experience with a girl. Don't worry; I got better over the years.

Youth football and my last year of middle school were great experiences in my life that taught me a lot about myself and what I wanted to attain in life, but they never prepared me for what came next. High School.

High school was a very strange experience for me on many levels and although many people may have seen this cool confident guy all those years, I was just trying to find out where I fit, like everyone else. Growing up I always had my closest friends at school with me and for the first time I was alone because they all went to the other high school in town. I had also never had many black kids in any of my schools while growing up, so now going into this very diverse school I had a lot of social dynamics to learn, and fast. Back then it wasn't like it is today and there wasn't a ton of segregation, but there was enough. We had students who would drive the parking lot with confederate flags hanging on their trucks, and we also had the thugs. So being the "Oreo" kid I didn't really know where to fit in. I wasn't white, although I grew up in a white family, so I didn't really fit in well with that group. I never grew up around ANY black people so I didn't really get the culture or understand it at all. So I would get made fun of for not understanding the slang terms or what they were talking about, and again I slipped into that feeling of a lack of acceptance and didn't know where to fit in. Until I happened upon the one thing I knew was a level playing ground for me, the football field.

Yet again I stood on the field where I found myself just one year earlier. This time it was different though. This time not only did it give me freedom, it gave me an understanding of where I stood with my peers. I don't care who you are in high school, if you're a good athlete, odds are you get accepted by everyone. So here was my chance to earn my acceptance and make a name for myself. I went out for the team and although I had sucked the year before, I had gotten much better in the offseason by practicing a lot and learning the game better. My work had paid off and it was noticeable. I could catch a little better, I could run a little faster, and I could hit a little harder. I started getting friends fast and some of the insecurities of not fitting in with the racial crowds diminished. When my first game finally came, it was time to show the school and my classmates what I was made of.

I remember the first game like it was yesterday. We were issued these faded poop brown pants with a white belt, a black jersey with holes in it, and an old helmet that smelled a little but fit perfectly. I suited up in all of my football gear and walked onto that field nervous as could be. I wanted to throw up. All I remember about that game was one play and how it stands out in my mind even now. I lined up as a wide receiver to the far right side of the formation, two yards from the goal line in a sprint position with my right foot planted firmly in front of my left.

My baggy jersey hung off my skinny body like I was a human hanger. I saw my quarterback Frank snap the ball as I took one step forward with my left foot, then my right foot came forward and I made a cut inside to my left on a slant. As I looked up I saw the ball heading straight for me. I put my hands between the ball and me, as I got ready to catch the pass. And BOOM, I had just caught my first touchdown pass. I was ecstatic. I went on to catch two more touchdowns that day and all of a sudden I was the star of the freshman football team in one game.

I wouldn't know until the next week that I wasn't ready for that, and honestly, I am glad I wasn't because it led to my next defining moment that solidified how I wanted to live my life. On top of just "wanting" to be great, because "wanting" is something everyone has, I had achieved something few ever experience in life and I will lay out in this next story why that is.

The very next week everything changed. For some reason I felt that I had a huge weight on my chest to perform after one good game. I had some of the prettiest girls in the school talking to me and I had all my teammates talking to and about me. The coaches showed me love. All was well and then I dropped a ball in practice. It wasn't a big deal, and I just brushed it off but it stuck with me for some reason. The next day I dropped a couple more balls. I started to get down on myself and it took a toll on my confidence. The little voices started creeping in also. "Are you sure your as good as everyone thinks?" "Can you handle all this pressure?" "What if you drop a ball in a game?" If you are unfamiliar with how the mind works then this is good for you to know. Whatever you give your mental energy to, it usually plays itself out in the real world. SO the very next game I dropped two touchdown passes and everything came crumbling down around me. I didn't have all the love from everyone anymore. I heard the snide remarks in the hallways. At practice I got ridiculed. Then it happened, the knockout blow.

I was running a route exactly like the one I ran to catch my first touchdown in my first game three weeks earlier, and the ball went right through my hands AGAIN. Another drop. Before I could even stop to pick up the ball five words were yelled from one of my offensive lineman that broke the camel's back. "Trucks, you've got fucking butterfingers!"

Internally I was demolished. I might as well have handed in my helmet and jersey right then and there because the rest of the season was a wash. The words he spoke were so detrimental to me because I was already down on myself, and now it was clearly apparent that no one cared about me again. I had fallen from grace and I felt the full impact when I finally landed on the solid ground of my reality. I started to question if I wanted to play football anymore. I started to wonder if it was worth having all these people judge me and put me back under their shoe to mock and laugh at. I figured it would be much easier to just hide away under a rock somewhere and stay out of their sight so they couldn't belittle me anymore. That was my solution. Hide away and not let my light shine anymore because of what other people had thought about me, and how I let it affect me. Yes I had wanted this so badly for myself, but I wanted more not to be ridiculed and subjected to that form of peer pressure.

Then I had my second epiphany and defining moment that linked with my first to create a fierce drive, unlike any I had ever experienced before. I realized that no matter how bad I wanted to be great at football, I had to work my butt off to get better at it. I was TIRED of listening to what people thought about me, or what I could/couldn't do according to their judgment. I had spent fifteen years of my life listening to the world tell me I was worthless, a waste of a human, and destined to be left behind by society. All that mattered to me now was what "I" thought of myself, and my capabilities. I paired those two thoughts and *lit a fire so deep inside my body that I have yet to find anything on this earth capable of extinguishing it.* I no longer cared what other people thought of me, and that mindset now freed me and gave me the ability to do something that I now felt I HAD to do. WORK MY BUTT OFF TO TAKE WHAT

I WANTED FROM THIS WORLD THAT HAD FOR SO LONG TAKEN FROM ME. I had learned through my own life experiences that the only way to get what you wanted was to work to achieve it, because no one is going to give you success. They're too busy looking for it themselves, and sometimes taking from you to attain it for themselves.

That offseason became the most important offseason of my life and for good reason. It allowed me to show MYSELF what I was capable of, and it allowed me the first opportunity to do what I believe we all need to learn to do—trust yourself, and ultimately **Trust Your Hustle**. If you take nothing else from this story, take this. You must fight to achieve something great at LEAST once in your life; to prove to yourself that you CAN trust in yourself to be successful. You OWE it to yourself to take that leap at LEAST once so you can see your amazing potential. So what did I do you ask? Everything I could think of! Not a day went by, literally not one day, where I didn't have a football in my hand. I carried it around school, I threw it up in the air and caught it at least 500 times a day, I slept with it, I never let it out of my sight. I wanted to have my hands be so use to it that when it was away they felt naked, and the only fix was to have the ball in my hands.

I ran routes at a nearby park with my teammate for hours every day that I was able to. I worked out at home as much as I could to prepare my body and. My dad, who is a welder, made me my very first dumbbell to workout with, a dumbbell that I still have to this day at my gym. I became so internally driven and cared so little about what people thought of me that I never even desired to tell people what I was doing to prepare. I wanted something even greater than me to tell people how hard I had worked and how much better I had become. I wanted the words to escape their lips, not mine. I wanted to show up to hell week the next year a completely different player who people couldn't believe was the same person from the previous year.

The next year finally arrived and it was time to see how my hard work in silence had paid off. It didn't take too much time for my statement to be made. I showed up to hell week a completely different athlete and person. I was faster and could outrun everyone. I was stronger and laid menacing hits on people. I was all around better as an athlete, and I was mean. I caught every pass. I was a tackling machine, and I could not be stopped. What I had worked for was coming to fruition. People clearly took notice of this new player that was killing everyone on the team and, as desired; I didn't have to say a word. There is this saying that when you think you're good you tell everyone, but when you're great, they'll tell you. It seems I must have been great because I heard it all over again, but this time it was different. I wasn't doing it for acceptance, I wasn't doing it because I wanted everyone around me to think of how great I was, I honestly no longer **cared** what they thought about me, good OR bad. There was one thing deep down that was driving me, that still drives me to this day and allows me to be successful at what I did then, and what I do now. I had endured too much suffering over the years at the hands of my elders and peers, and I had decided to be great regardless of what had happened. I just needed to work harder than I thought I was capable, to PROVE it to myself that I was worthy of my dreams. When that realization was solidified from my offseason work, and it WORKED, I would not allow myself to be beat. Not even on one single play. EVER. This is the trait that has made the man the world sees now.

Now I know what you're thinking, "Everyone says they won't be beat." Yes, but does everyone put those words into action? The reason I was so mean was because I had gone through so much in life and I had literally fought too hard throughout life and the past offseason to let ANYONE take away from me what I had rightly earned; my right to be great. It didn't matter what anyone said to me now. I now controlled me, and I now knew what it took to be successful. I learned in that instance in my life a great truth that I want the entire world to learn. It doesn't matter how many times someone tells you that you can do something, or you say it out loud to yourself. You must get to a point where you accomplish a great feat and you **intrinsically** create a fire inside from a burning belief and personal KNOWING that you harbor what it takes to achieve greatness. You must EARN YOUR OWN TRUST in order to trust your ability to do whatever you set your mind to in life. Having someone like me telling you is NOT enough. It also doesn't matter what the world deems "big," it just needs to be big enough for YOU.

Nothing of any great importance is earned without great effort and struggle, and that's how it should be. Everyone is capable of greatness, but I do not believe everyone is worthy of it. I believe you must earn your right and worthiness to be great through the sacrifice that great men and women go through to achieve it. I believe EVERYONE is capable, but not everyone is willing. Once you have earned this right to place your mind and heart amongst the greats, you no longer question if you can be successful and reach greatness; you EXPECT it of yourself in everything you do. It's an earned mindset change.

From that point forward football for me took on a life of its own and I continued to improve year after year, even after being brought up to varsity as a sophomore that year. Even though I was continuing to give my all on and off the field to achieve greatness, I was still fighting the struggle that every teenager fights off the field; growing up and learning from good and bad experiences, and good and bad people. My high school years were never dull. I have had my fair share of run-ins with bad decisions. In high school I had my first experiences with drugs, just marijuana. Within a three-month period I smoked weed five times and it was the last time I ever did so. I hate the feeling of being high because I cannot focus and it makes me feel as though I am not able to do what I do so well, be mentally strong.

My brother, who is a person I now look up to with great pride and respect, almost died in a park bathroom from drugs and it changed my whole outlook on substances. My brother means more to me than I will ever be able to place into words and that time of my life it internally scared the crap out of me because I almost lost him. I started hanging out with guys who cared more about drinking and partying than they cared about me, and it led to some bad decisions. I threw some parties at my house that should have never happened. I started to slip off into the deep end and there were a few things that were able to wrangle me back in; some good, some bad, and some sad.

When I was a sophomore in high school something rattled our family that still affects us all to this day. My mom had recently finished getting licensed to be a nurse and she was working at the hospital down the street. I remember how proud she was of her accomplishment and how hard she had worked to achieve it. She had five kids and was able to manage to take care of her schoolwork and become a nurse. One day I was standing in our kitchen and I saw a look on my mom's face that I can only describe as sorrow mixed with fear and dismay. My mom was trying to complete the simple task of feeding herself with a spoon but to her surprise she was unable to get the spoon into her mouth. Most people can feed themselves with their eyes closed, but she was staring at the spoon and could not find her mouth. She had limited control of her own body. At work she was no longer able to give shots because she could not control her hands anymore. She went to a doctor and was diagnosed with Multiple Sclerosis or M.S. for short. Her world was shattered because everything she had worked so hard for was ripped away without a moment's notice, and the fact that it is incurable makes it even more devastating. Here is the woman who has given so much of herself to her family, and we were helpless to help her. To make matters even worse we kids didn't realize the severity of the situation until years later and sadly we probably did more damage than help during the early years of her M.S.

My dad is an amazing man and has stayed by my mom's side through more ups and downs than an average human being could handle in a lifetime. Although he may not know it, he is a testament in my eyes to what a love for your spouse should be. He has modeled love and support in ways that deserve a medal.

I managed to fall into horrible habits at school and out of school. My sophomore year I failed a couple of classes, I started hanging with some unsavory characters, and as soon as I got my driver's license I took an even further detour. You see, although I was a good kid at heart who had a goal in mind and was able to work hard enough to afford a car and a cell phone, I was still a kid and I made mistakes, one that almost cost me my future entirely. Before I was able to get too deep in, however, I met someone who changed my world forever, in a good way. Around the age of 16 years-old is when I was in the middle of my "rough patch." I was out driving my car around and I met up with a friend of mine who introduced me to a girl named Tanya. I wouldn't know it then, but this girl was going to save me, from myself. At first Tanya was just a friend of friends and nothing more. The more we hung out the closer we became. Tanya had the most infectious personality you could imagine. She stood tall in stature and confidence. She had an amazing body, she was a decorated athlete, she was funny and had a great laugh, she was beautiful, joyful, very smart, driven, warm, and she had a smile that could melt your heart. She was a mix of Puerto Rican and Pilipino and stood 5'8" tall with a beautiful olive complexion and shoulder-length dark brown hair with a hint of burgundy if the light hit it just right. She was everything I could have ever wanted in a girl and more. I didn't know until later but the feelings were mutual.

The more I hung out with Tanya the more I hated time away from her. We would always talk on the phone, text, running up our text bills, hang out after school, hang out on the weekends, and before you knew it, I struck gold and we became a couple. It was odd because I never did ask her out, but we became an item. Over time we struck a bond stronger than any I had ever experienced. I know people say that at that age you don't quite know love, but I would challenge that belief with every ounce of my soul because at the age of seventeen I was deeply in love.

Although I had this great girl in my life now, I was still making stupid decisions. For some reason I got into breaking into cars at night. I don't know what it was about the thrill of it, but I had some strange addiction to the feeling I got when I did it. Looking back I am disgusted beyond measure at the horrific things I did to other peoples' property for my own selfish thrill. I wish I could go back to every person who had to wake up the next morning to see their property damaged and apologize from the deepest depths of my heart. I was acting idiotically and my actions were inexcusable.

Everything came to a head at the age of seventeen when I was at a house party and made the stupidest and dumbest decision of my life. I had a good job working for my grandma's office as a janitor, I had an amazing girl-friend, I had the respect of my coaches for football, and I was receiving letters from colleges wanting me to play for them almost daily. I was popular and my parents were proud of my accomplishments, and I had EVERYTHING to lose. So what did I decide was a good idea? Going out to break into someone's car. Tanya begged me not to go, liter-ally begged me. I remember her taking me aside, looking deep into my eyes and begging me not to go again. I prom-ised her it was the last time, and although I didn't believe it when I said it, it would be the last time. She stormed out when I told her I was still going to go.

I had this feeling in my gut that I shouldn't go but I didn't listen to it. I left the party with two other guys and went to one of their houses to wait until it was a little lat-er in the evening. At about 1:30 a.m. on a Saturday night I drove my car to a nearby house where one of the guys knew the person with the car had a subwoofer system that we were going to steal. I parked my car a block away in a court; we all hopped out and ran to his car. When we got to the car we shattered the back window and that familiar rush came crawling back though my body. We were wear-ing dark clothes, breathing hard, sweating, and moving as fast as we could with a rushed feeling that is unexplain-able. After about two minutes we had freed the item and were running back to my car. We got in; I started the car, and we sped away as fast as we could. The rush was gone, and the feeling of elation crept in behind it. The scariest thought was getting caught in the act, so once we would get away free and clear, we could finally settle down, but the shakes follow for hours. We had done it; we had gotten away Scott free and were in the clear. Or so we thought.

I drove back to the house we had been at prior to making the trip. We then examined the goods and I left everything at the house with one guy while I drove the other guy home, because I had to get home. I went back outside to my car, started it up and drove away. His house was about five minutes from my house, which meant taking the main road to get to my house. As soon as I entered the main road heading home I saw a police car fly by me with no lights on. I drove a little ways up to see the car make a left. It just so happened that I had to make a left as well, so I did. I then saw the lights on the police car make a right. I didn't think anything of it, but I also was going to be making a right. If you have already figured out what was going on then you are smarter than I was at that moment. I continued to drive myself home and as I rounded the corner to my house I saw parked across the street from my house the very same police car. As I approached I saw the police officer ten steps from my front door and when he noticed my car, he started running back towards the street. I slammed on the gas and made a hard left at the next street three houses down. My blood froze and I was in full-blown panic mode. I made the very next left at the street below mine on the block and pulled into a court about half way down the street. I turned off the car and lights and sat in a cold sweat praying that he wouldn't find me. He had already seen my distinctive white car and I happened to park under a street light like a genius. Not even thirty seconds went by before I saw the car slowly creeping by, shining its white spotlight around the streets before it locked onto my car. The car swerved in front of my car now nose to nose and the lights flipped on.

I was in a world of fear. The police officer shined the light directly in my face and with his microphone instructed me to place both of my hands on the steering wheel. He then instructed me to place them outside of the window and open the door slowly. By this time the neighbors had started to peek out their windows and proceed to stand on the lawns to watch everything unfold. As I stepped out of the car I could see one thing that scared the shit out of me; a black pistol aimed squarely at my face no more than fifteen feet away from me. "Get on your knees and place your hands behind your head!" I knelt down and placed my hands behind my head. It was about this time that the next two police cars arrived to aid in the situation. One officer drew his weapon and slowly approached me with a gun point blank in my face instructing me, "Don't move."

The officer came around, grabbed both of my wrists, forced me to the ground face first, knelt on my upper back and proceeded to place my hands in cuffs behind my back face down in the gravel. After being picked up, I was lead to the police car, patted down, and put in the backseat while they proceeded to search my car.

I remember being so embarrassed due to the number of people watching; people who knew who I was. I was now sitting in the back seat of a police car with my head hung down as the police ransacked my vehicle. There was nothing in my vehicle as I had not taken anything with me, but there were many incriminating tools that all but assured them of my guilt. Then one thing happened that shook me to my roots. A police officer had found a stack of my college letters inviting me to play football at their school on a scholarship. He went into the front passenger seat, placed the stack of letters up against the mesh between the front and back seats and spoke five words that I can still hear. "You can kiss this goodbye." Up until that moment I didn't think it was possible to hear the sounds of a future disintegrating. What had I done?! I had failed my family, my girlfriend, all those who respected me, and most importantly, myself. I had become what I vowed only two years earlier that I would never become at any point in my life, the polar opposite of great. I had become the statistic of what a child who experienced my life was assumed to be, a criminal. How could I have been so dumb? What was I thinking? How selfish of me to do this to my sick mom, loving girlfriend, and my future success.

After what felt like days, after the sun had already risen and the neighbors had gone back inside, the police completed their search and I was driven to the police station where I was booked and placed in a holding cell next to two individuals who looked like a future me if I continued on the path I was heading. The afternoon my aunt Anne came to pick me up and I remember not even being able to look her in her eyes. I slunk out of the police station, got into the car, and started the shameful drive home to see my mom Grace and dad Mike; who were so disappointed they couldn't bring themselves to be the ones to pick me up. When I arrived my grandma Barbara's, Grace's mom, who had given me a job, was at the house as well. I walked through the door and saw everyone in the room waiting on me. I sat down on the black couch and received the scolding of my life, which ended in me going up to my room for the entire day and not even being allowed to eat that night. I locked myself in the room and was alone with my thoughts.

What had I just done to my family? My future? My girlfriend? My life? Why didn't I just listen to her when she said not to go? The next day I was taken back to the police station to speak with the officers. Upon arrival I was taken to a room and asked to sit down. With me were my parents and my grandma, along with the arresting officer and another officer. The officers went on to explain how they found out so quickly where I lived. I tried to lie and make up a story about what had happened to protect my friends, but they weren't buying it. Apparently a neighbor had watched us park the car near the house of the people we robbed and wrote down my license plate number. They then proceeded to follow our car and watched where I dropped off my two friends. They then reported it to the police who responded, and the rest was history.

The police already knew where my two friends lived and actually drove me in their police car past their houses to prove to me that they knew. We were all doomed and it was my entire fault. Yes, they had the choice to go or not, but I was the one who drove and it was my idea. I had affected so many lives negatively by my horrible actions. I went home after the meeting and drive, and went straight back to my room.

I had now been off the grid for a couple of days and my friends and girlfriend were starting to get worried about me and came to my house to see if I was O.K. My car was impounded so wasn't in front of my house, and my parents didn't want anyone knowing where I was, so they told my friends I wasn't home.

* * *

I had now come to another defining moment in my life. What do I do next with my life? Do I slither away and drop under the weight of my guilt, or do I choose to pick myself back up yet again and try to make something great of myself. I had all but lost everything. Trust from my parents, my grandparents, my coaches, my friends, and I had no idea if I would still be able to go to college. Earlier I stated that it was a good and bad thing that happened. It was good because it stopped me from proceeding down a slippery slope where I was apparently heading, and it forcefully re-corrected my path to the one I am STILL on to this day, thirteen years later. I decided to pick myself up and make a success of my life once and for all.

An angel gave the strength to move on. The only person I couldn't stand being away from was the only female I had ever let deep into my heart, my girlfriend, my angel, Tanya. The look on her face after she saw me for the first time made me feel so bad, yet so loved. She didn't hate me. She didn't judge me. She unconditionally showed me love in my most trying moment. She supported me because I believe she knew the person I was deep down. I had made a mistake, and she stood by my side to help me correct it. At this pivotal point in my life I had dug myself a hole. I was involved in drinking, partying, and I was failing three classes and had no idea how to get out of the hole. My girl-friend at the time was a 4.0 model student, so I followed her lead. She helped me dig myself out of the deepest hole I had dug for myself.

Without proper grades, the police officer was going to be proven right, I would have to kiss my opportunities goodbye. After talking to my teachers I was allowed to go back and make up all the work I needed to do in order to bring my grades up. I had no idea how to even do most of the work, sadly, so I needed a tutor. For 6 weeks straight, every night I would go to my Tanya's house and she would meticulously break things down for me and teach me how to study, how to complete my assignments, and how to simply be a good student. I had NEVER been taught this in my entire life. After six weeks of getting home af-ter midnight each night from studying, I got caught back up in school and was now eligible to accept a scholarship. She saved my future by her kindness and ability to love me unconditionally, even though my faults. How many 17 year-old girls would/could do that?

I fell in love with Tanya. The first time I ever told a girl that I loved her was when I was sitting in the passen-ger seat of her grey Nissan car. We were about to pull out of her driveway to go with some friends. I placed my left hand on hers as she was about to shift into gear, stopped her, looked into her eyes, and told her that I loved her. I could hear my heart beating so fast, but to my elation, she returned the words and my heart swelled; I was locked in. There was no one else on this earth meant for me to love. From that point forward I made it a point to be the absolute best person I could be, and make every single person I was around proud to know me, and most of all myself.

I was now coming close to ending my high school years and after my ordeal I needed to get myself back to a feeling of being worthy to attain what I wanted out of life. My grandma Barbara allowed me to go back to working for her again, although she was reluctant at first because her employees might have been a little distrustful of me cleaning their offices at night. My grandfather Tom, who had taught me so much when I was attending karate under him, allowed me to work for him at the house he was having built. That summer would prove to be one of the times in my life. I learned to appreciate what hard work does for you mentally, instead of complaining like most people do. In my experience, when someone is given a hard task, his or her immediate thought is to get out of it, whereas in my life now, I eerily like it because I get to test my gumption and see what I can muster out of myself to earn success. To me it's a fun test. That summer I was left alone day after day in the heat to do backbreaking labor and landscaping. Some days I would be left alone to shovel and take rocks in a wheel barrow from the front yard to the back yard for up to 8 hours. I had to plant plants, shovel manure, you name it, and I did it. I would get to work at 7 a.m. and be there until I got off at 3 p.m., which gave me just enough time to get to summer football practice that started at 3:30, which entailed lifting weights, running, and hours of practice sometimes. The truth is, I never complained about it. My grandfather is a very demanding ex-marine who wouldn't allow me to complain about it, and that priceless lesson he gave to me.

I now am beyond thankful for the lessons I learned that summer about what kind of hustle and hard work it takes in silence in order to be successful at what you want in life. No matter how many people can voice the words to you, you can never learn that lesson until you have sweat every drop of sweat from your body and been proud to do it under those harsh terms.

The next year was my senior year in high school. By this time my brother had fully cleaned up his act and, after graduating, enlisted in the Navy leaving me behind to make a life for himself. My mom's M.S. had escalated so quickly that she was bound to a wheelchair. I was the talk of the school with all the scholarship offers coming in and coaches visiting the school to meet me. I had the love of the most beautiful girl, inside and out, that I had ever met in my life. I was set. Football season is the first sport of the year and I had made sure I prepared better than I ever had before to be ready to make my senior season the best ever. I didn't disappoint. In my first seven games I had fifteen sacks, twelve touchdowns, and lead the league in tackles.

One huge driving force was my mom Grace. Since she could no longer walk I was to be her legs, and she was going to be able to live vicariously through my actions on the field. Every time I scored, I would point up to the sky and although everyone thought I was only pointing to God, I was in fact pointing to my mom as well. It was our thing. Sadly, one game she was too sick to attend. I went to an away game in a local city and I played tremendously, having three touchdowns in the game, and every time I pointed to the sky like I always had. The next morning, on the front of the local newspaper, was a full-page picture of me holding the football in one hand and my finger pointing to the sky with the other; for Grace and God. So although she wasn't able to see the game, she knew she was still in my thoughts at those moments. I still have that picture in my office to this day.

We would go on to play a powerhouse school nearby called De La Salle and we got pummeled 63-0, and then boom, my season was cut short. I had broken my left wrist and that was the abrupt end to my season. A feeling of horror fell over me. Will I still be able to get a scholarship if I am hurt? Is my future that seemed so bright gone once again? I was filled with an unshakeable fear.

I tried my best not to tell any teams about the injury and for the last three games of the season I was able to hide it. It wasn't until the season was over that I felt safe, but that was short lived. About this time I was getting numerous calls from schools all over the country. I received calls from Nebraska, Oregon, USC, Utah, Michigan, UNLV, and more than 50 other schools requesting recruiting visits. I still had a cast on and I hadn't told any schools so I postponed them as long as I could.

Then came my very first recruiting trip to a college. I hopped on a flight that took me to?? Upon arrival they saw the cast and didn't seem to worry at all. They said I would be healed in ample time to play, so it was a non-issue, and I was so relieved. That, however, wasn't the end of my dilemmas and experiences on that first trip.

Upon arrival I was paired with a current athlete on the team and shown around. Now this is where it gets sketchy. I am a man of sound morals and beliefs and no matter what happens in my life I will never do anything that will make it hard for me to look myself in the mirror every night and not respect the man I am looking back at. With that being said, cheating on a significant other is one thing I would never do in this life or the next. With that in mind, I will fight to make sure none of my children EVER cheat, and I won't even consider you a friend in life if you do something so disgraceful. My disdain for cheating runs deep and I was now thrust into an unfamiliar world. I was in a college, with college girls, and college parties. That is a recipe for disaster for an impressionable young man being treated like a king on his recruiting trip. I was walked into a party, shown four girls and instructed to pick which one I wanted.

Like divine intervention someone happened along my path at that very moment that saved me. This person happened to be on the team and knew me from high school. He talked my recruiting host into letting him be responsible for me the rest of the night. He took me out of the party and we went for a walk. After about a half an hour of walking and talking we ended up at the stadium of this college. He had access and proceeded to open it up and lead me in. We walked to the top of the stadium and sat there in the snow- filled seats overlooking a beautiful landscape of the college and talked about life. He happened to be a very solid man internally, with strong morals and beliefs, and he was the perfect person for me to be with that night. We talked about my girlfriend, college life and how it gets crazy, and mostly about the need to be a sound, grounded person when I choose a college in order to succeed when I did get in.

I don't believe anything happens by accident, and this chance meeting was no accident, someone planned it. I ended up committing to go to Washington State

University, and I was more excited than I can remember. The feeling of acceptance when I announced my decision to the team was amazing. I couldn't wait to call my parents and my girlfriend and tell them the good news. They were ecstatic! I hopped on a plane and headed home, all the while thinking about my future, what it would entail, and my future teammate's words of wisdom that essentially boiled down to the fact that I needed to be a solid person inside if I was to succeed in college and life. Something unique happened that night. At the airport I was picked up in an old airport van taxi by a man in his mid-40's who looked almost like Jesus; with a scruffy beard, long brown hair, and a navy blue beanie . He drove me home, about an hour and a half trip. I truly believe that nothing is by accident and this man was proof of this.

On the way home from the airport all this man did was preach to me. At first I didn't care to listen, but as time went on his passion and knowledge captivated me. Little by little I started to feel this odd feeling that something was stirring in me. Then I stepped back in my head and started reflecting on my life and all the things I had experienced; the fact that I was in a car driving back from the airport after visiting a college t I would now go to for free to play a game I loved. If that wasn't a higher power watching over and guiding me, then I didn't know what it was. His words rang true in my ear that all I have and all I will become is from God. All trials in life are a bigger design to make me the man I am and will become. All the strength I will ever need to drive past pain and turmoil in my life will come from only one source, God. I was about to embark on the scariest new chapter of my life and I was not solid inside. There is absolutely no way that this man and my future teammate were put in the places they were at those exact times by accident; it was a sign.

I had always been raised around the belief in God, but it was not emphasized. As I got closer to my home the man stopped on the side of the street a block from my home. We happened to be parked on the corner of the street where I had been arrested. He proceeded to pray a prayer that seeped into my heart for the first time ever. He prayed for me to accept Jesus Christ into my heart as my Lord and savior. This was no accident, and neither was my life leading up to that point. I believe I am part of a bigger plan that God has for my life, and although I am FAR from a perfect Christian, as you will learn as my story continues to unfold, I have a deep rooted base of Christian morals and beliefs that drive my life. There is no way I could have gotten where I am today alone.

My senior year flew by after that signing day in February when I, in a twist, de-committed from Washington State. The recruiting coordinator for the University of Oregon would not leave me alone, and I eventually changed my mind and decided to sign with the University of Oregon. I took the recruiting trip on Nike's private jet, and fell in love with the school so much that I changed my mind on the spot. The coach at Oregon called me every almost morning and every night. He wanted me so bad that he continued to call even though I had told all the other schools I intended to sign with Washington State. Obviously his effort paid off; he apparently knew how to trust His Hustle.

I had garnered many accolades in high school and I was voted first team all-league as a wide receiver. I was top 10 cream of the crop in the bay area, and was respected by my peers. I ran track and did very well. I was a phenomenal long and triple jumper and almost made it to state. I was fast, but not faster than my teammates who ran the 4x100m race. I really enjoyed running track just for the simple ability to be able to hang out with my friends and my girlfriend, who joined her senior year to spend even more time with me. She actually was a great athlete herself and was awarded senior athlete of the year.

Another cool thing is that I was voted homecoming king. Every year our school chooses a senior to be Mr. Panther, our version of the homecoming king. It is a position that is chosen by the student body, and peers choose candidates. Once chosen, all the students vote on the final nominees and those six people hold skits to show off their skills and hopefully win the vote. I was paired with a man, who is now one of my very best friends in life, and we chose to do a skit of the fast and the furious, where we would also have our own "showcase" to let the student body see our skills. His section was a Latin dance where he had five couples go out and dance to salsa music. At the last minute one of the guys didn't go out, so I sprinted in to dance with the girl who was dancing alone; and butchered the dance. My section was a solo dance by me to a song called *Let it Burn* by Usher. I went out in a one-piece high-end jean suit and proceeded to take my shirt off and have my girlfriend Tanya dance in front of me. Let's just say it was fun for both me, and the girls in the stands, or so I was told.

That night the student body voted while we all got dressed up in our suits as guys, and our dates got dolled up in their dresses to attend the basketball game. I must say my girlfriend donned the sexiest gold dress I had ever seen and I was proud to have her on my arm. At half time everyone stood to hear who won and they called my name. I honestly couldn't believe it. I was the LAST person I would have expected to win, but it was an amazing honor for a guy who had gone through all that I had endured in my life. I am thankful to this very day to everyone who voted for me because although I didn't live to have everyone's acceptance of me anymore, it is still flattering to know I was accepted and loved by the majority of my peers.

To make things even better, my amazing girlfriend and I were voted the cutest couple for the yearbook. In the yearbook we actually had a picture together wearing our one-piece jean suits. I was literally on cloud nine.

Then out of the blue I got a call from someone I hadn't spoken to in four years. It was my biological mom and she had somehow managed to get my cell phone number. My heart sank and I became flooded with emotions that I hadn't experienced in years. She tried talking me into giving up on dreams of college and move in with her in her trailer park home in Jacksonville, Florida. My heart almost burst with the overflow of emotions ranging from empathy to pure anger. She had called to tell me that she needed a new kidney and only had six months to live if she didn't get a donor. This person was literally the only person who could stir up the emotions in me and I felt like a young child all over again. I didn't know how she had even gotten my number. Obviously I refused her the new kidney, and come to find out, it was a bold lie. She was back to her old ways of making up lies to get me to believe them, but I was now too old to put up with her lies. I asked her to never call me again and hung up on her.

As senior year came to a close and all the graduation festivities ended, a sad reality started creeping into my heart; I was going to have to leave my girlfriend who was going to attend a local college. My heart hurt at the thought of leaving her. I had grown to love this girl more than I loved anything else in the world, even myself. I would literally die for this girl. I remember laying in her bed one night while we held each other, talking about what we would do. Would we continue the relationship, or just break up? We both knew it would be easier to break up, but we couldn't bring ourselves to go through with it. We decided we were going to stick it out and fight for the relationship and do the "long distance" thing. Although we had already decided to stay together, the pulling feeling of having to leave soon never left our bodies and we couldn't imagine being apart.

Much to my mom's dismay I spent every night of the three weeks leading up to leaving in late July at my girl-friend's house. I would fall asleep holding her and in the middle of the night, drive home so that I would be there in the morning when my parents awoke. My mom almost never saw me and she was already missing me, knowing I would be going off to college soon. She pleaded for me to stay home more often, which only resulted in my girlfriend and I hanging out at my house more often. I am the only child of all six of us to go to college, so this was and is still, a one of a kind experience for my mom. All I could think about was how much I was going to miss my girlfriend, my friends, my family, and the amazing life I was living at that very moment, but the only thing constant in life is change.

So on one fateful day I packed up my car, my parents packed up theirs, my girlfriend came along for the ride, and we started the drive to Eugene, Oregon where the next chapter of my life would take place. I remember driving away from my house, passing the street I was arrested on, then driving down G Street near my house, and passing Milner Street where I used to deliver newspapers. As I passed the familiar houses I realized this was the last time I would ever call this distinct place home. I was about to embark on a journey of life much grander than I had ever imagined while growing up. The realization of where my life was headed was upon me, and as I drove out I thought about the newspaper photo of me with one hand up at the game for my mom who was unable to attend the game. I signed it, "I'm going pro baby" and purposely placed it in our school's time capsule for our graduating class.

I was going to make it to the pros, or at least make something great of myself. It was now time for me to say goodbye to the town that raised me, and greet the world ahead. I did so with the first set of happy tears I had ever cried in my life. With my girlfriend seated next to me, I pressed the gas on my car, and my life, and continued on.

CHAPTER 5:BOYS TO MEN

In college, unique things happen. You go from being a boy to a man. You arrive with a wonderment and are introduced to a freedom unlike you have ever experienced before. Then, if you're lucky, you graduate with tools that you can use to start your adult life, from both formal and informal education. After an eight-hour drive I arrived in Eugene, filled with excitement. It was a place I would most likely spend the next five years of my life, away from anything or anyone I had grown to know over the years. My girlfriend and I, and my parents, all stayed for about a week visiting the local scenery, college coaches, and the college facilities where I would spend the majority of my time.

Then on the final day I was ready to check in for fall camp for the new football players. My parents loaded up their van while my girlfriend and I said our final goodbye in the parking lot. With tears streaming down her face she could barely breathe. I had to hold it together because I was about to walk into a room full of football players and the last thing I wanted to do was arrive with wet eyes, although I could have easily let a few roll. I gave her the biggest hug I could and let go. Then gave her a final kiss, turned my back, and walked inside to greet my future.

Fall camp, or training camp at any level of football, is hell on earth. It's hot, you don't know anyone, you're getting yelled at by coaches, you're mentally tired, physically tired, and all you can think about is how uncomfortable you are and how different it is than coming from high school where you were a king on campus. Many players going through this horrible experience get homesick and can't wait to leave. I must admit it sucked for me to be away from everything and everyone, but I was here to make a future for myself., and honestly, change like this wasn't all too far from what I had experienced for years while growing up, so I had a leg up in that area on most guys. Nothing could compete with the added fact that my position coach was hell bent on making our lives miserable while we were there. We had to be early to everything, do everything perfectly, and he didn't give us ANY wiggle room. We had to be perfect, or be perfectly on time for the 6a.m. punishment for messing up. Let's just say I hated him then, but in hindsight I love him for having the gumption and desire to build young men with structure; giving them the life skills necessary to be successful in life, although they may not know it at the time.

Years later I had multiple conversations with him, thanking him for being as hard as he was on me. He told me that it was his job. Parents leave their kids with him and he makes sure when they leave, he has made them a better football players, but more importantly, better men.

My freshman year was a flurry of experiences, both on and off the field. On the field I was working my tail off, like I always did, and it was paying off. As. freshman we were expected to sit out a year and do what's called "red-shirting," where we learn the system, then come in the next year. But I wanted to play now! So after three games of sitting out my coaches gave me the go to get on the field. We were playing Portland state and I got my first chance to get on the field in kickoff. As a true freshman who had only played football on a varsity high school team prior to this game, I was stepping into the big league. Division 1 is the highest level of football in the world below the NFL, and I was now about to run down on kickoff in a game. I could feel the anticipation surging through my veins as adrenaline boosted the beats of my heart so much I could probably have felt my ear lobe throbbing. I lined up with one hand down and, as the kicker approached, I sprinted as fast as my legs could carry me on a collision course with the kick returner to the sound of 60,000 screaming fans on my home field in Autzen stadium.

One of the coolest things about this time in my life is that my dad, my grandma, and my uncle would make the trip for every home game, and in fact they witnessed that first play. I remember looking back at my dad and catching his proud eyes as he saw me making the move to the field. My dad would work until 4a.m., then they would load up and drive 8 hours just to sit and watch me and, "possibly" get a chance to play in my first game." I still cannot express how grateful I am for the kind of actionable love and support they showed for me during those times. I sat the bench for all of those early games and they were right there with me. So when I finally got the chance to go in for my first play, they were there watching and I couldn't have been happier.

So there was this young 18 year-old boy weighing no more than 190 pounds who had a heart about to beat out of his chest lined up and ready to run full speed, 40 yards down the field, and try to make a tackle on his first college play ever. I was the first player on the left side of the kicker. As I heard the crowd noise rise in my ears, I saw the kicker begin his approach. As he got closer to me I raised my hips, turned off my brain, and sprinted as fast as my body could travel I heard the wind speeding through my helmet as I saw the player setting to block me. I avoided him and locked onto the ball carrier as soon as he caught the ball. The kick returner veered away from me and, like a cheetah running down its prey, I flew in and made the tackle; solo. It was my first play and first tackle of my career. I became addicted to that feeling of triumph and the sound of the crowd cheering from my accomplishment. I knew I was capable of doing this exact thing over and over again, and in fact I did for the next four kickoffs in that game. My very first appearance on that football field landed me five solo kickoff tackles in five kickoffs. No one else made a tackle on kickoff that day but me, the new guy. This was the start of something beautiful.

* * *

At the same time I was doing my best to keep up my performance on the football field, I was also living a college life that had some interesting dynamics. I had classes just as everyone else did and I was buckling down to complete the assignments, just like I had learned from my girlfriend. I had recently received a letter from my biological grandma that said she and my mom had moved up north of me, near Portland, from Florida. Something raised an alarm inside me, but it wasn't anything that shook me enough to lose sleep over it. Mostly I missed the heck out of my girl. I think that my lack of motherly contact and a real mother's love while growing up, caused me to developed attachment issues with her. I loved my adoptive mom with all my heart as my mom, but a girlfriend is different. She would visit every one to three months and on her first visit back, I remember doing something that few 18 year-olds ever think of doing. Leading up to my girlfriend's first visit back we had some rough patches. The phone calls were full of longing and sadness, and she wasn't strong enough to fight through the rough patch, so much so that one night she had her best friend call me to tell me she wanted to break it off. I cried and begged her not to. I was able to get her mind back on track and I told her something that I was fully able to follow through with. I told her that someday we would look back on this time of our lives and laugh at how we acted. We will see this as one of the many points where things could have gone wrong, but we were too strong of a team to let it go wrong.

I went to the local mall and used every bit of money I had to buy Tanya a diamond ring so small that you could barely tell it wasn't just a gold band. Then I drove Tanya to a place that overlooked the entire city of Eugene. We parked and got out then walked up to the rail and gazed out over the fall colors and beautiful town below. My heart was in my throat as I was about to ask this truly amazing girl to spend the rest of her life with me. I pulled a tiny black box from my jacket pocket, opened it and turned to face her. On a cold dusky afternoon in September

I asked Tanya to marry me. September 2nd 2002 to be exact. She said yes.

Please keep in mind that at that very moment I was locked in to this decision for the rest of my life, I had zero inhibitions. I KNEW I wanted to spend every last moment of my life with her. In fact, my teammates used to laugh at me saying I was silly to think I would be able to keep this girlfriend throughout college, because no one lasts so I may as well break it off immediately and explore. I was determined to make them eat their words. I would talk to my parents about once a week, and when I told them they were happy for me.

The next few months included some fast-paced decisions and a lot of teamwork on our parts. After that visit in September she went back home to check-in to her college. One weekend on a season bye week the coaches gave us Friday-Sunday off because we didn't have any games that weekend. So I had an amazing idea; what if I made a surprise trip to her school eight hours away? She didn't seem to like it there very much so I wanted to cheer her up. If you are familiar with the northwest in the fall/winter, then you know how tough a drive in the middle of the night can be with the cold, wind, and pouring rain. I didn't care; I wanted to see my fiancé. I hopped in the car without a second thought and was on my way.

I arrived at her dorm before she made it home. I met one of her roommates who allowed me in and let me hide behind the door. After a couple minutes the doorknob started to jiggle then unlocked, and in walked Tanya, my fiancée, to see her roommates sitting on the couch opposite of me with creepy grins from ear to ear. She took a glance left and leaped like a kangaroo into my arms hugging me so tightly I could barely breathe. EXACTLY the welcome I had been looking for. We spent an awesome weekend together, off the grid because not even my parents had known I drove down. This is definitely a memory I have held onto forever.

After the holidays a great idea spurred in both of our heads and hearts. My fiancé hated her school and the major she wanted was actually offered at Oregon because they happened to be ranked second in the country. I was tired of being looked at as an a-hole at Oregon by the girls because I didn't give any of them the time of day or even say hi because I didn't want to even remotely be involved in something that would jeopardize my relationship. Believe me, in a co-ed dorm, that opportunity was possible 24/7, especially being on the football team and actually playing. Tanya was tired of the long distance relationship and so was I. How about we just have her move up to Eugene? An idea that was smart and stupid at the same time because she had nowhere to live. My roommate was a great guy who was actually from nearby my hometown. He agreed to something that I am sure has to be illegal. He let my girlfriend move in with us in our itty bitty dorm room so she could attend school. Even my R.A. somehow was cool enough to let this go down. It worked out perfectly. She moved in and we started our journey together at the age of 19. The whole dorm experience was uneventful until I received a call from a random number on my cell phone one day and answered it.

The phone call came from my biological mom Molly and, let's just say, things hadn't changed. She still wanted me to stop playing football for some odd reason I still cannot figure out to this day, and her crazy stories spewed out like yesterday's garbage, only I wasn't the garbage man picking it up anymore. Somewhere in the conversation I was introduced to my biological grandma on the phone, and it was the first time I recall ever talking to her. After talking for a while the conversation turned. It was a sunny afternoon and I was sitting on the 6th floor of the dorms at my desk with my girlfriend looking out the floor-to-ceiling window that overlooked the college. My girlfriend leaned over my shoulder listening to every word when the conversation finally changed to my biological father.

Over the years my mom would scoff at the idea of talking about my father and she always used to tell everyone not to call me Tony because it was my father's name, although the birth certificate said Daniel. My grandma alluded to my father and in one instance I latched on to the topic, even though she was reluctance to talk about it. She said that my mom made her promise to never talk to me about it because my father was a horrible person. After a little coaxing from my girlfriend to keep pressing the issue, which I actually didn't want or care to know, my grandma eventually broke and told me my father's last name. For privacy of my father and his family I will not disclose that name, but I will tell you it is a Nigerian name.

I was floored. I had for the first time been given a key to a locked portion of my very base of existence. Thanks to my fiancé's steady persistence and forcing to beg my grandma, I had the name of the man who shared my blood. So many thoughts ran through my head. Should I not call out of respect for my dad? Did this guy really abandon me and should I call angry? Did he even know I existed? Did he even care? I had watched so many movies up to that point that depict how a meeting of long lost family members could play out that the possibilities could have been endless. Before I got ahead of myself, I had to first find the man though. At this time in 2003, the Internet was fairly new, but there were resources that allowed someone to type in a name in a web based name directory and search it out.

My amazing and caring girlfriend and I, mostly her, found out that my father lived in a small town in Georgia, and there were only five people in America with that last name. To my luck this website actually produced a working phone number for the person who shared my first name and this last name, hence the "don't call him Tony" statement my mother perpetuated for so many years. The phone number was typed into my little black Nextel phone and my finger hovered over the call button as I looked up nervously into my girlfriend's eyes. She said "do it" and the phone began to ring.

My heart was pounding with the angst of not knowing what to expect on the other end of the line. Would he hang up? Would he even know what I was talking about when I asked him questions regarding the past? Should I just hang up now? "Hello?" said a voice with a deep Nigerian accent.

"Hi, is Anthony available?" I asked.

"This is Tony" answered the man.

"Hi Tony, my name is Anthony Trucks and I was wondering if you have a minute to talk?"

"Yes I have a minute, who is this?" he asked.

"Well I wanted to know if you would possibly remember a woman name Chelsea from Martinez?"

"No, but I knew a woman named Chelsea from concord," the man answered. What you'll need to know to make that statement make more sense is that in California concord borders Martinez.

"Did you happen to be dating her in 1983?' I asked.

"Yes, she left me because she said she was pregnant with an Italian man's baby."

"Well my name is Anthony and my mother is Chelsea and I was born in December of 1983, in Martinez and I think you may be my father. My mom always told people not to call me Tony, and my birth certificate has an Irish name on it, but I happen to be black and she is obviously white." The phone went silent for a minute, and I could almost hear the gears turning in his head. The silence was only a couple of seconds but it felt like an eternity because it was now the moment of truth. What was he going to say?

"I guess that makes sense" he said. "I tried to go see the baby at the hospital but she would not let me in the room." The conversation went on for a while and it actually went in a positive direction. He had no idea I existed as his son, and this entire time I thought he was a horrible person who left my mom to raise me alone. I was mistaken. He spent almost the entire conversation apologizing for not being there as a father when I needed him. As I told him my story he continued to apologize for not being there. He genuinely was angry at my biological mom and the fact that he didn't know he had a son for 20 years of his life, and that he wished he had known so he could have helped raise me.

Knowing all of this took a huge weight off my shoulders. He actually accepted me as his son without any further questions. I got to learn about his life, his/my family, and what he'd been doing over the years. I also filled him in on my current life and what I was up to and he was proud of me for accomplishing the things I had accomplished in life I then found out I had a step mom, an older half-sister and a younger half-brother who were also gifted athletes.

We talked for a while and I even got to speak to my step mom on the phone. They are amazing people and it was great to be able to close up that hole in my life. We ended the conversation on a good note and I felt as though I had a little piece of my life completed in simply knowing where I came from, and knowing that my father wasn't the horrible man my mother made him out to be.

Soon after talking to my father my freshman year came to an end and I moved out of the dorms with my fiancé. We moved into a duplex with a teammate and my cousin, who had moved up from my home area. The upcoming year would prove to be a unique one to say the least. I had a fierce desire to start as a true sophomore, which means I would have to take the starting spot from a senior, and that wasn't going to be easy. I literally gave everything I had to prepare that year. I learned every single play I could, I took risks, and I NEVER gave up on a play. Not very often does it happen, but after a hard fought battle I won the job after what my position coach called one of the best position battles he had ever seen in a camp.

My first start was to take place that year away at Mississippi State in Mississippi, which happened to be only five hours from where my biological father lived in Georgia. So I called Tony and invited him to the game so I could meet him. He agreed and in the next couple weeks I would be able to meet my blood father. So many things had to line up for this chance occurrence to happen; such as the school I chose, my ability to play and start, and the fact that we were going to play a team that we had never previously played away in the school's history. This was meeting meant to take place.

I remember how nervous I was leading up to this game because it was going to be a nationally televised game, and it was going to be my first college start. I was also going to have the opportunity to meet my birth father and the other half of my family for the first time. The game was a night game, which meant I had to sit around all day with these nerves. I had spoken to my father the night before and he told me he would be making it in some time in the afternoon and wondered if it would be possible to meet me at the team's hotel. I said yes and gave him the address. I remember not being able to sleep that night because of all of the thoughts obviously spinning through my head.

I awoke the next morning ready to take on the day. We had morning meetings to refresh and go over the game plans for that evening, then we were given a large break in the middle of the day to rest and watch some other teams that were playing. I sat in my room on the edge of the bed watching a game on TV when I received the call from my father. My heart stopped as I answered and heard him say, "We're downstairs." After hanging up the phone I called Tanya and shared with her the news; I was moments from meeting my father. She shared my excitement. I couldn't think of anyone in the world I wanted to tell more than her. I seemed to float as I glided into the elevator and downstairs.

When the elevator door opened, there stood an older, dark Nigerian man about 5'10" tall with a light-skinned black woman standing by his side, along with a young boy and a college-aged woman. I couldn't believe this day actually had come in my life. A grin carved itself in my face from ear to ear and I hurried over to give everyone a hug before walking outside with everyone to talk. It seemed like hours, but in fact was only about 30 minutes. I was in shock the entire time, as I could not fully accept the situation that was at hand. Somehow God made this meeting possible that day. After a long, warm conversation with them, we shared in a final embrace and I went in to prepare for the game while they went to the stadium to watch me play.

When game time approached I was ready. I was about to don the Oregon jersey for the first time as a starter, in front of millions, and in front of my family I had just met. The game proceedings took what seemed like an eternity as I awaited my chance to step onto that field to play. My first college start began with a kickoff where I honestly do not remember whether or not I made the tackle. What I do remember is that the nerves spiked and disappeared after my very first play. It was time to go, and I was the starting outside linebacker for the University of Oregon in Mississippi, as I had been in little Antioch not more than two years ago before heading up to college. The offense made its way out to the field as our defense prepared for them to line up. As the strong side linebacker I found the tight end and made the strong side call. I made my way over to the tight ends sides, got into my alignment, waited for the snap, and BOOM. The play seemed to be over in a flash and the nerves had disappeared. The same feeling I had when I first began football seemed to rush back to me all at once and I felt in control of myself, and my desire to play at full tilt. I was on fire like I had been through-out camp. I made my calls and made the plays. I was on national television and my biological family was there to watch it all happen.

One play that stands out to me is a play where I lined up on the left side and the offense snapped the ball, leading into a pass play. The running back flared out left and I saw the quarterback turn to throw him the ball. A soon as I saw the Quarterback turn his body to throw that direction, I shot off like a bullet on a demolition path for the running back. The moment he caught the ball I laid into him with everything I had, sending him flying backwards. It was a culmination of all my pent up nerves being transferred to his body in one loud "crack" that seemed to act as a trampoline on our sidelines. Everyone was hopping up and down from the amazing hit I had just laid on him. I had arrived. I made my presence felt, and this was only the beginning.

After the game I was honored to receive the special team's game ball for my outstanding play. So on one very memorable night I was able to meet my biological father, start for my first time in a division 1 college game on national television under the lights, and play so well that I received a game ball. The world was opening up for me. Then, as quickly as it opened up, it closed.

Two games later we were playing against Washington State. As I lined up on the right of the formation, the ball was snapped and a wide receiver came down from my right side to crack block me. I stuck out my straightened arm to stop the blow, and instead it blew out my right shoulder. It wasn't an immediate pain, and I honestly didn't feel it right away as my adrenaline was high, but the next day it was apparent something was wrong. My fairytale story came to an abrupt end. I managed to stick it out and try to play with one arm for six more weeks, but the pain was excruciating and I couldn't even manage to brush my teeth with my right arm anymore.

I had to hang up the jersey that year and get surgery. My world collapsed as my dreams of grandeur came to a screeching halt. Would I ever be as good after I recovered? Why didn't my coaches want to talk to me anymore? Who was I without football? Thankfully the same awesome woman in my life who was instrumental in organizing my ability to meet my father was there to support me, and love me unconditionally through this trying time. She was my rock and handled the situation like a pro at the tender age of 19. Not only that, but she gave me the internal strength I needed to keep pushing towards my goals of being great, and made me realize this was just a speed bump on my path to success, not a wall. After surgery I would be on a long road to recovery, a road that would itself have many bumps along the way. To make things worse, one morning I awoke to find my car had been stolen. When it rains it pours I guess.

* * *

In March,, 2004 I received a call that would change my entire life forever. It was a typical March afternoon and I was about to start my afternoon football workouts. I went to the bathroom then checked my phone before heading to the weight room. I noticed a few missed calls from my fiancé, so walked to the back door of the locker room where I then called her back and got an earful of what sounded like tears. "What's going on? Are you ok?" I asked. Her next two words have had a profound impact on my entire life ever since.

"I'm pregnant" she responded. My mind and heart stopped, so much so that you could have heard a pin drop. So many thoughts rushed through my head all at once as I turned silent for one of the few times in my life. I didn't know exactly what to say, I was in shock, but I will tell you this, I was FAR from sad or worried. I was a full time student and full time athlete, she was a full time student, and we were in another state without any family support. But my first feeling about this situation at the age of 20 was jubilation. I was going to now be able to provide a life far better than my own for someone else. My very own child! She wasn't as excited as I, but it was not due to a fear of having a child with me, it was more due to the fear of the having a child at the age of 20.

I had a feeling of fear and resolve all at the same time and I knew we were going to be great parents. I was willing to do whatever it took to be a good father, and I loved her more than life itself. She had a job and was going to school, while I was a full time football player. So how were we going to handle a newborn baby on top of all of that without any help or support from our families, and still be successful at reaching the goals we had set for ourselves? The chips were definitely stacked against us, but I knew that as long as I Trusted My Hustle it would all work out somehow.

The next nine months were crazy as we prepared for the baby to come; all while still attending our sophomore year of college. Some things could not be prepared for, and one happened to be the deaths of two of my close grandparents. One of my grandmothers passed without notice and it was a difficult one to swallow because she was my great-grandmother, my mom's grandma, and I loved her so much. She had always been there over the years. The second was my close great-grandpa Erin. What made this one worse was that I was privileged to talk to him one last time while he was on his deathbed. I remember getting a call from my grandma one night in the summer of 2004 telling me that grandpa was on his last leg. The last time I spoke with him I was riding with my fiancé in the back of a friend's black dark grey 4-door sedan as we went with him and his girlfriend to eat ice cream at Prince Pucklers in Eugene. We parked out front of the ice cream shop and they went in while Tanya and I stayed in the car so I could talk to him. When he spoke, his voice was so faint on the phone I could barely make out his words. But I can still hear them as he simply said, "I am proud of you, and I love you." All I could respond with was, "I love you too." I hung up and knew it was the final time I would ever hear his voice, and a flood of tears streamed down my face. I grabbed for the red hat I was wearing and covered my face as my pregnant fiancé leaned over and gave me a hug. My grandpa was a great man and Navy veteran, and his birthday that year would have been on November 3, 2004.

Amazing things happen in this world every day and I was able to experience one later on that year in 2004. It was mid-season of my junior year and I was just a 20 year-old kid starting as a linebacker for the University of Oregon. As I was sitting in a meeting room around 3p.m., watching game film to prepare to play against the Cal Bears, my phone rang. I was the only one allowed to have my phone on in the room as I was waiting for "THE CALL" that would let me know it was time for my baby boy to be born. I remember it vividly when my phone rang and it was my fiancé. My eyes bugged out and my heart rate climbed as I told my coach I needed to step outside to take the call. I answered the phone and my fiancé simply said, "It's time." Now the crazy thing is that she's a trooper and at 3 cm she was in fact driving over to pick "me" up from the practice facility, to then go in and have her water broken to have the baby.

"YES!" I yelled from the hallway before I stepped into the meeting room to tell my coach, who apparently already knew from my outburst. I grabbed my backpack and ran out to meet the mother of my first child. We hurried to the hospital while on the phone with her mom, telling her to hop on a flight immediately. My future mother in law had purchased an emergency ticket and all she wanted to do was be there as the baby was born. We arrived at the hospital and the doctors got the process going immediately; and they weren't waiting for her mom.

Leading up to the birth, Tanya actually felt no contractions until she was 9 cm, and then received an epidural to numb the pain so she might have felt 3 contractions throughout the entire birth. At 7:20 she started pushing, almost the exact moment her mom came through the door. At 7:41 p.m. my son Anthony Mack Trucks was born into this world as the most loved child this world may ever know. His birthday happens to be November 3rd 2004; the exact same day that would have been my late grandfathers next birthday. God showed his greatness in that act for my family.

Not only did we push ahead as a team, but did it damn good if I must say so myself. We made a great team. I went back to normal the very next day as we had to go away to play Cal that weekend, and she was back to school on Monday. Our schedule was like clockwork and we made it happen like pros without ever needing a babysitter or daycare. My fiancé had our schedules locked in and she even did my entire academic advising, getting me into classes that helped us keep our schedule, and eventually helped me graduate. I would get up at 6:40 to get ready for school to take the 7a.m.-12p.m. classes. Later I took the bus straight home to watch my son as she went to her classes' midday. Then she would return at 2:30 so I could get to my 3p.m. weight lifting, followed by meetings and practice that would end and get me home around 8p.m. every night, usually with a fruit smoothie that I would make and bring home for her, and then I would either have to stay home or go to study hall. When I finally got to stay home I would take my son off her hands while she finished her schoolwork and/or went to late night classes. .

We had this schedule down pat and we made it work for three years from the ages of 20-22. This child never went without either of us and he will not know until he is older how much love his parents have for him. Not many teenagers can have and raise a child with all even with a support system, let alone no support system and busy lives like we had. But we managed to do it with flying colors. I kept right on with school and my fiancé actually earned a 4.2 G.P.A. that quarter after going right back to school five days after having our son. This is when I first got the deep seeded desire to make others' lives better than my own, because of how great it felt to give to my son. That seed would eventually grow into a great thing in the ensuing years of my life.

College with my small family couldn't have been any better. We spent countless Tuesday nights at Pizza Pete's eating all you can eat spaghetti. It was a low-key, laid back place where the waitresses knew us from how often we came in. The spaghetti wasn't the greatest, but it was all you could eat and the bread was amazing. We also went bowling with all of our friends, who were mostly athletes, which meant having some of the most competitive bowling games you could imagine, but all in fun. During this time poker was huge on TV and online so we would have poker tournaments with our close friends. My fiancé's cousin and his girlfriend moved up to Oregon with us and we spent countless nights playing poker. We actually held a few poker tournaments at my apartment lounge and invited tons of people to donate to our winnings. We had a blast just hanging out and playing the game with friends and family. We would play the Newlywed game at our house on boring evenings. The funniest thing is that one time two of our friends, who weren't dating and had only known each other a little while, beat every one of the four couples playing that night. The other random thing we decided to get into seriously was playing pool at our friend's house. Somehow he had managed to get a pool table erected in his upstairs living room that left barely a two foot clearance all the way around, and we would spend hours eating over at his house, playing pool until we couldn't stay awake any longer.

As a small family in college we made time to do a lot of fun things together. We explored thrift stores for random knick-knacks, and odd things. You never knew what you were going to find and that was where all the fun arose. We found movies for $1.50 where movies from the big theaters would go. Imagine a little run down movie the-ater that showed every movie you had seen in the big box office not two months prior all for as little as $.99. When that wasn't enough we would resort to watching movies on a 10' sheet with an overhead projector at our house, with all of our close friends over.

Solo nights with my fiancé and son were the most memorable and fun. We had a blast-playing scrabble for hours on end and keep track of who was winning. I hold the record at eight straight games won. No matter what I reflect upon during my college days, my favorite times as a group with our friends took place during Friday night dinners at the Arcadia house. This was a house owned by one of our friends that had three other girls living in it. We would all go over to the house on Friday nights and just hang out and have our own little parties. It was perfect for our son because he could just hang out at the house with all of us. To me it was more fun than any nightclub I have been to in my life. I wouldn't have changed my experience in college with my son or fiancé for anything, because we managed to have an amazingly memorable time over the years.

Those memories all paled in comparison to my most favorite moments in college; the moments where I was a father. Around the time my son was born, Snoop Dog had come out with a song where he added "izzle" to the end of words so, like typical college fashion, everyone got nicknames ending in "izzle." So I was now A Tizzle. The reason I bring this up is because my son soon after assumed my name, and his name was modified to be Mack Tizzle, instead of Anthony Mack Trucks. He in fact thought his name was Mack Tizzle for a few years before he understood his real name. To this day, I rarely ever call him by his first name, instead he's "Tiz."

From the day he was born and I slept in the hospital next to him for the very first time, I was in love deeper than I had experienced before. I loved just holding him and hearing his breath, his smell, his everything. How could someone not love his or her own flesh and blood? This is something that I still can't fathom. In the beginning it was hard staying up late with him while he cried, and early mornings when he wouldn't go back to sleep. I would have to sometimes endure the entire day on minimal sleep.

One Christmas Eve night I stayed up with him while he cried the entire night and by Christmas morning I was a zombie. The truth is I wouldn't have had it any other way. I never complained because I had learned two things. 1) I knew that nothing in life of any worth would come easy, and 2) It was an amazing bonding time for my first born and I. Tizzle is my little man, and he always will be.

We also had out normal firsts, like his first steps which happened at eight months, which is very early for a child; the day before he and his mom would drive home for the summer while I checked into training camp for a month. As he got older it seemed like a daily dose of joy just watching him grow. His smile lit me up daily and I loved just coming home to spend time with my family. We would all cuddle up on our broken in brown couch that was to this day the most comfortable couch I ever owned. We got Anthony his very first dog, a chocolate lab named Hershey, but the management didn't allow it and we had to give him away, which was O.K with me because he peed on everything. We had a playground outside of our door and I remember how amazing it was the first time tizzle climbed up the slide backwards. Being an athlete, I was the proudest dad ever to see my son's skill. We never worried about him falling so he got to explore his body and his environment freely, which allowed him to gain great body control and athleticism. I am sure I will be remembered many ways as a man on this earth, but the only one that truly matters to me is that I am remembered as a loving father to my children. I am most proud of being a father and the fact that my kids will grow up happy, healthy, and never have to experience what I had to endure.

The next year was to be my last year in college sports, and I was going to make sure all remembered it. I wanted so badly to make something of our life in any way possible, and I wanted my child to have so much more than I was ever given. Growing up without my blood family in place was something that made me want nothing more in this world than to have my family in place forever. I wanted to be that old man who is the head of the household overlooking all his children and grandchildren and loving them to pieces. This foundation would only be laid with faithfulness to the woman I loved, always keeping in mind the people I was doing it for. That mindset drove me to prepare beyond my comprehension for my final year.

When my senior year arrived I was on a collision course with a great that season. I prepared like no other and got both my mind and body in the necessary shape to take on the upcoming season. I had caught the eyes of the upper ups and I was actually blessed enough to be put on a huge billboard that was displayed over the city of Eugene. The season started out strong and I was killing the competition. I had three phenomenal games and then I hit a snag.

I suffered a high ankle sprain that forced me to have to sit out against the USC Trojans, who were highly ranked and would have been a great game for me to showcase my talents. No matter how hard I tried to run I was unable to. I ended up being able to play the next game and the rest of the season, but I had to do so with three ankle braces and a walking boot any time I wasn't at practice. So I would play in games and dominate on Saturday, and then walk around campus in a boot the entire season. It seems that for me whenever everything is going well, something has to pop up and make sure I remember that everything cannot be great all the time.

My senior year we went down to play the Stanford Cardinal in Palo Alto and I was excited because all of my family got to come and watch me play. I had two sacks and a lot of tackles, so you could say I had a great game. After the game I was excited to get dressed and go see my family. I rushed to get showered and out to the buses so I could visit before my team had to get back to the airport to fly home. I walked out of the locker room to see all my family, but instead of seeing happy faces, there was a somber feeling and faces of sadness. I didn't know what was going on but before I could speak up, my brother Miles grabbed me and walked me off to the side to talk to me.

"Anthony, I don't know how to tell you this, but Grandpa Frank took his life last night," I was speechless and my feeling of elation after a great win was immediately deflated. I didn't know how to respond. My grandfather who was the happiest jolliest man I had ever known, and who was the Christian figurehead of our family, had committed an unthinkable sinful act and I couldn't understand it. My heart felt so full of sorrow it seemed to weigh down my entire body. I went back to my family and gave everyone hugs and thanked them for coming out to the game. Although no one wanted the focus of the day to be negative, there was definitely a solemn feeling residing over our visit. Everyone wanted to wait until after the game to tell me, and for obvious reasons.

I barely remember the flight home and I was mentally stuck the entire week after. I held in all of my pain and shrugged it off like it didn't matter to me because I felt I had to be strong for my son, my fiancé, and my teammates, because it was the middle of the season. A week later I couldn't hold it in any longer and right before practice one day I walked up to my coach's and asked if I could go home because I needed to let it out and grieve. I went home and cried to my fiancé and I was able to let out my pain and move forward; accepting the situation for what it was, a learning experience, and a loved one lost. Everyone has demons and I guess my grandpa's burden became too much for him to handle anymore. We all wish it didn't happen, but I don't love him any less.

After I was able to gather myself and move forward I managed to complete a phenomenal senior year of football. I ended up leading the Pac-10 conference in sacks, tackles for loss, forced fumbles, fumbles recovered, and I was six in total tackles, all while missing the game against USC earlier that year. A funny memory comes to mind about this year. One of the biggest college football rivalries is the Oregon vs. Oregon State Civil War game and it was to take place at Oregon my senior year. When I was a senior in high school I attended a football camp at Oregon State and I weighed in at 183 pounds. My coach told me I would never play linebacker at the division one level. That game ended in me leading the team in tackles with 13, 3-pass hurries, and an interception. I received the defensive game ball in that game by dominating our rivals in the last game I would ever dawn the Oregon colors in Autzen stadium.

Yes, my last game at Autzen was great, but it was only great because of what it meant to me to be a Duck, and the amazing experiences I had there. There is nothing like coming out of the tunnel in Autzen stadium. We would leave our locker room by exiting through a door that was basically a wall that lifted up in two seconds to reveal our entire team. We then would walk down our tunnel and hear the echo of a mixture of our cleats hitting the ground, our loud yells in angst, and the best sound of all;

the stadium full of our cheering fans awaiting our arrival. We walked down the tunnel in a mass of bodies, and the feel of having the team at your back was indescribable. Every step brought me closer to the bright opening at the end of a dark tunnel. As we neared the entrance, the energy flowing in from the crowd was palpable. I was always the leader and as soon as I stopped at the front of the tunnel, my fellow teammates stopped behind me in what must have looked like cattle ready to burst from the gates. Anticipation for the game could be heard by every man's voice behind me, and I couldn't wait to run out onto that field.

My last game in Autzen was nothing short of the greatest experience to date. We were on our home turf ready to take on our rival in a game that would help decide our fate in a possible BCS game. So the anticipation of taking that field was greater than it had ever been because I did not want to have my last game on my home field be a game I lost. So when I stood at that tunnel opening, my heart was full of all the emotions one would expect. Fear, anticipation, pulling, excitement, and so many more feelings filed my body.

The next moments of the tunnel are the moments that can never be recreated or matched in any form in this world, unless you happen to be an Oregon Duck about to take the field. With 100 men ready to take the field in front of a sea of green and yellow, out bellows a roar that shakes the walls of the tunnel and increases the yells of the crowd tenfold. Oregon has a Harley that rides out leading our team at every game with our mascot seated behind the driver. When that engine turns over, chills ride down your back from head to toe that is nothing short of a human earthquake. Every nerve ending in your body tingles as all your senses come alive to take in the amazing experience.

You can feel the vibrations of the engine in your entire body as the pulses repeat with every rev. Your eyes look around and catch your teammates' eyes who share the same look of eager anticipation before they pan out to look upon 60,000 + screaming fans who have also heard this roar. They are now on their feet jumping and stomping while they pump their fists and arms with pure excitement. You can smell the engine exhaust pair with the smell of the stadium and all its glory. The excitement and energy is something that is literally palpable and can be tasted. There is nothing like this moment on God's green earth. Every sense is overloaded at intense levels. I felt every hair on my body stand straight up, my blood courses faster and faster as my heart rate increases. Every muscle in my jaw flexes as I clench down on my mouthpiece with full force. My muscles feel like they're going to burst if they don't start to move, and then it happens.

The motorcycle revs its engine, pops the clutch and

flies onto the field as I explode out behind it, as fast as my body can take me while I lead a sea of my teammates onto the field. In between, our cheerleaders make a V on the field for our entrance. Out comes a yell that is usually reserved for the fall at the top of a rollercoaster; a feeling of emotion and energy being pushed from my body in one climactic moment. It is time to take the field with my brothers in a game that is a blessing to experience. It is the purest form of release in sports and nothing can recreate the amazing feeling a player has exiting the tunnel at Autzen stadium.

Our team finished 10-1 and we were invited to play in the San Diego Holiday Bowl against Adrian Peterson and the Oklahoma Sooners in December of 2005. It was the last time I would ever play as a Duck and I wanted to leave a mark. I played my HEART out and it showed. I stripped Adrian Peterson at the goal line and stopped them from scoring. I led the team in tackles, and I physically dominated their team, play after play, because my heart was in every play. We ended up losing by three points, but I played so well that I received the award of defensive MVP of the game, even though we didn't win the game.

After the game I was so dismayed that I ran off the field before I knew I had won the honor, and I didn't find out until I read it in the newspaper the next morning over breakfast with my family in San Diego. I also made the U.S.A. all bowl team where after all bowl games are completed, they vote on the best players by position. I signed with my agent that very evening after the game, and I would soon be off on the next journey of hopefully entering the NFL.

After signing with my agent I was shipped off to Scottsdale, Arizona where I would train for five weeks to prepare my body to perform at the best of its ability for my pro day at Oregon in March. I hadn't played well enough to get an invite to the NFL, so I was going to get one chance to show what I had. I got to Arizona at 6'1" weighing 213 pounds and looking to play linebacker in the NFL, where most guys weigh between 230-260lbs. So to say I had some work to do would have been an understatement. All I knew in my life was success through hard work and effort. This to me was just another stepping stone on the path to greatness that was in need of my unique skill of being able to tackle and accomplish large tasks. I went in to this journey full bore every single day with my sights solely set on preparing myself to be the best athlete I could be. I worked myself so hard that I was close to throwing up during my workouts every single day; I ate as perfectly as I could imagine a person could, and I stayed strict to my regimen of sleep and recovery.

Two weeks before I was supposed to go home I was given a late invite to the 2006 NFL combine in Indianapolis and I was JUICED! After five weeks, I left Arizona and flew to Indianapolis to attend the 2006 NFL combine. I was 233 pounds, bench pressed 405 pounds and jumped 37", and was able to run a 4.51s 40-yard dash. I was ready.

Upon arrival to Indianapolis, I took the Cybex test, a test that measures leg strength and KILLs your leg muscles. I went in to eat with a room full of guys I had never seen before, and who were probably as nervous as I was to be there. After finally getting my room assignments I went to my room to meet my roommate and found my clothes for the weekend laid out on my bed. My roommate happened to be a muscle-bound black guy about my height, who wasn't a very talkative individual. In the NFL this is common to have to spend the night in a hotel room at workouts and tryouts with guys you had never met prior to checking in. The next morning we woke up to head to breakfast and physicals. We were taken to a room where they took our picture, without clothes on, then sent us out to the hallway. The physicals were comprised of eight rooms with four teams of doctors in each room representing a different NFL team. I would walk in and be asked to take off my shirt and lay face up on a table. Each doctor would grab a limb and start yanking away to see if I had any instabilities or physical problems. The worst part is that they didn't even call us by our name, only by a number. So I had to remember that when a monotone voice yelled

"Linebacker 32," it meant they wanted to speak to me.

After the brief exams, where I literally felt like a piece of meat, rather than human, the doctors would sit me up, huddle and go over their results, then report their results to the panel of people sitting in front of computers. I remember one doctor stating that I had an injury to a body part that I, in fact, did not have, so corrected him, only to be scolded for speaking. After that I had seven more to complete. After the 8th exam I was sent out to a local hospital to have MRI's completed, which ended in me spending four full hours in MRI tubes that day, trying to be as still as possible without falling asleep or jerking awake; then I would have to possibly redo the MRI, and that would have been horrible.

The day spent in the MRI tubes cut in to my ability to complete the 225 rep bench press test, so I would have to make it up at 6a.m. the next morning, which was in fact like 3a.m. to me since I was coming from the west coast. After the bench press test, where I pressed 225lbs 26 times, I was escorted to a room and told to strip down to my underwear and step into a room where I was to enter something called a bod pod that would take my body fat measurements. Once I exited the bod pod, I was ushered to a line of men against a wall in their underwear. The bleacher seating set up was filled with NFL coaches, GM's, and other staff. Slowly but surely we would each move closer and closer to an uninviting stage. As soon as I reached the front podium a man grabbed me by the arm, turned me around and measured my hand and arm length before sending me up onto the heavily lit stage. Once on stage my name was yelled out loud and I was looking into a sea of silent faces. The lights were so bright I couldn't even make out a face. I was backed up against a wall where I was measured for my height by the most non-inviting man I could imagine, then asked to step onto a scale that was directly in front of a large screen that showed my weight to the audience. I was now standing in a white pair of underwear on a brightly lit stage with at least 100 grown men staring at me like I was part of the cattle ready to be sold at market. Then the word "finished" was yelled and I was told to walk off the stage and get dressed. I headed back to my bag and put my clothes on. Day 2 completed; 1 more to go.

On the third day we woke up and headed downstairs to meet our group leader to be taken out to the field to finally perform the drills that the public actually gets to see on TV. We reported at 6a.m., to walk out to the field to get warmed up then put through the drills. I went out with a group of about forty linebackers who were all fighting to outdo the other. We warmed up as a group really quickly before taking some measurements for flexibility. We were then let loose to complete our own warm ups before running a forty in front of millions of people on TV, and hundreds actually present. One by one each person went in successive order until it was now time for the 32nd linebacker to run his 40, and that meant me.

I walked into the end zone, undressed, said a prayer, and approached the line. As I walked up I could see that all the faces in the building were on me. What most people don't know is that on TV it looks empty, because you can't see the stands full of bodies, or the massive amount of people- seated at the 40-yard line holding a stopwatch. I walked up to the white line on the black field riddled with divots from cleats; made by the previous guys who had used this line before me to show the scouts how fast they could run. I took a knee and set up my feet, placed my hands on the line, buried my head, and waited to lift up my knee before taking my run. As I sat there with my head buried and my cleats laced up as tight as possible, all I could hear was the sound of my heart beating loudly against the silence of hundreds of people. A feeling of fear mixed with anticipation emanated from the very depths of my soul, and against every feeling in my nervous body saying not to move, I lifted up my knee, took a deep breath, and shot out with every single ounce of strength I had pent up in my body. What seemed like forever only lasted 4.8 seconds, and just so you know, that was a VERY disappointing time for a guy who had run 4.5's his entire career. I sulked back to my bag and prepared for my second run. I didn't run much better on my second run, breaking into a high 4.7, which was by far not my best attempt to say the least.

I went on to jump an 11'2" broad jump, a 37" vertical, and some decent times in the L-Run and Short Shuttle drills. My roommate ended up running a 4.5 40, and bench pressed 225lbs 41 times and performed very well in his drills, which later ended up in him being drafted to the Titans in the 5th round. As soon as the drills ended I was placed on a bus and sent to the airport where I would take the long trip back to Oregon and wait for my pro day in March to make up for my poor performance in Indy.

When I got home all I could focus on was making sure I followed through with my goal of making it to a team and that meant I HAD to improve my numbers. I spent every day putting in as much work as possible to prepare myself for my upcoming pro day where I would have a chance to better my scores and look good for the scouts. I would go down to the facilities and my fiancé would film my running so I could review it later and fix any issues I was having with my drills. I eventually felt comfortable with how I was progressing.

My pro day came and I was ready. I ended up running a 4.51 40-yard dash, I improved all of my times, and I was impressive looking to the scouts. I was then ready to take part in position drills. Pro days are similar to the combine, except much more time is spent doing position drills, but with less players so you have to take more reps more often, which can be very tiring. I was the only Linebacker from Oregon coming out that year so I was going to have to run drills alone, which was going to suck horribly. I was first asked to run a couple of the defensive back drills with the DB's. I took part in all of their drills, which was very tiring. After the DB's did their drills, next up were the defensive linemen, so I was going to get a break while they did their drills. WRONG. I was asked to partake in the D-Line drills and I just about died since I was already tired from running upwards of 40 yards with the defensive backs. We finished doing the defensive lineman drills and I was gasping for air and thirsty as could be. All I remember was hearing four words that almost crushed my spirit. "Ready for linebacker drills?"

With all I had in me I mustered up the strength to trudge ahead and line up for the linebacker drills. With a stone-like gaze and sweat dripping off of my nose, I dug deep inside my soul to push out whatever in me was saying I was tired, then applied the knowledge that I had learned about myself over the years—that if I trusted in myself to push hard enough, I could accomplish whatever I set my mind to. HIKE. I went over and over again with drill after drill, which took a little more out of me. By the time I had finished I was completely spent. My lungs felt like I was a dragon breathing fire, my hands quivered, and my body felt so tired I could have literally lay on the ground and slept right then and there. The final test was for my quarterback Kellen Clemens to throw 10 balls at me from 20 yards away, and see how many I could catch. I was so tired I literally only caught one ball; barely able to keep my eyes open or even control my hands. When it was all over, the workout complete, the scouts walked over and congratulated me on my display of work ethic and overall physical shape. One scout of note was the scout for the Pittsburgh Steelers who spent a few extra minutes talking with me and saying how he respected that I didn't back out of any drills and gave it my all.

When he left I lay on the ground and didn't move for at least 20 minutes, just waiting for my body to recover. Now it was the worst time in the NFL for a college athlete trying to get into the NFL, it was the waiting game for the draft.

The entire year leading up to this time my fiancé and I had been planning something huge to take place during this break time, before the draft, and it had finally become time. We had planned our wedding and it was going to be amazing. The wedding took place in Maui, Hawaii. We had invited over 70 people to join us in Maui for our special day and to our surprise we had over 60 friends and family attend. This week turned out to be one of the best weeks of my life. The day arrived for us to pack our bags and take the fateful trip to Hawaii. My son and soon-to-be wife were in tote as we headed to the airport from Eugene. I can recall the feeling of pure inner peace and impending completion. I was about to go on a plane and marry the person that I had absolutely no doubt in my mind I could spend the rest of my life with. She was my best friend in the entire world and I was indeed the luckiest man in the world to be able to soon call her my wife. No two people were more in sync in this world than us. We spent as much time as possible with each other and never tired of the moments, we could laugh together about random things for hours, and the thought of forever with her seemed like it wasn't long enough. My heart swelled with pride and I couldn't wait to look her in her eyes and put a ring on her finger to finally make her mine in front of my family and God.

We planned to meet up with our families in San Francisco at the airport when we landed from our short flight from Eugene. Our families are very unique. My soon to be wife's side of the family are very happy and colorful people. Her mom and aunts are some of the craziest and happiest women you will ever meet in your life, who could hang at any party and probably out drink most men. They were also professional women in their careers who knew how to balance it all. Her grandparents were two people that anyone in this world would be able to look up to. Her grandmother is a warm-hearted caring woman who everyone in the family looked up to. Her grandfather is one of the warmest caring men I have ever met; respected by all who knew him. My soon to be in laws are one of the closest families on this earth. My family was comprised of my half-siblings who made it a point to attend my wedding, my mom and dad, my older brother, who was my best man, and some of my closest friends in life. This trip was one that I could not wait to take.

We met up with our families at the San Francisco airport where we all hopped on the same flight to Maui. We landed in Maui and the festivities began. The flight might as well have been a party because we had so many of our family members on board. When we landed, my uncle and his wife who had been living in Maui, were waiting with Lei's for everyone. I remember traveling down the escalator and seeing their smiling faces looking up at us with a welcome sign and arms full of traditional Hawaiian leis. The week was full of amazing experiences that will always be rooted in a positive place in my heart and mind.

We got our rental car and drove down the highway with the windows down and a warm Hawaiian breeze flowing through the car as all three of us took in the feeling of peace and happiness on the way to our time-share condo. The condo was three feet from the water overlooking an amazing view of the neighboring islands. Every night we got to fall asleep to the sound of crashing waves against the brick wall in back of our condo.

The next few days included snorkeling, ATV riding, nights out with family and friends, and great food. Then the day arrived when I was to be married to my best friend in the entire world, and the idea of this made me so happy I could barely hold it in any longer. When the morning of the wedding arrived I awoke and looked out of my brother's hotel window, where I had slept that night, to see the wind blowing so hard that the palm trees were doubled over and not a soul was outside. My first thought was that there is no way this beach wedding could take place with that kind of weather, but who knows how it could play out by the time the wedding was to begin. I had all of my groomsmen and my brother there for support while I got dressed to head down to the beach. As we stepped outside it was as if God himself had opened up the heavens and shone his light down in acceptance of this union. The day was a picture perfect Hawaiian day with a slight breeze and sun that warmed us to your depths. Our souls were meant to be together, and this omen couldn't have said it any clearer.

I wore loose fitting beige pants that blew loosely in the wind, a white flowered short sleeve shirt, and a pair of dark brown Doc Martin shoes. Little by little all of our family and friends arrived and the 60+ seats filled up with familiar, smiling faces. The reverend made it a point to tell me that this was in fact the largest Hawaiian wedding he had presided over. He said it was rare for two people to have so many people attend a wedding who aren't natives, which meant we had to be very loved and supported in this decision to be married. Before I knew it the time had come to start my wedding and I was now realizing that I was in my final moments as a single man, and the thought of it was pure elation to me. I was proud beyond belief to be able to be married to this woman.

The music began and the ceremony commenced. I remember watching everyone walk out hand in hand and the anticipation growing with every new face. Then my handsome 2 year old son came walking out in his khaki pants and yellow flowered shirt, ushered along by my aunt towards me. The fateful song began to play and I knew it would be only moments before my beautiful bride would grace the ceremony with her presence. Everything around me went blank as I finally set my eyes upon her beauty as she rounded the corner with her grandfather, who had essentially been her father growing up. She was the most beautiful thing I had literally ever seen in my life that day. She wore a white strapless dress that showed off her amazing body; her dark brown hair styled in a way that made her face glow in contrast to her smooth olive skin. Her smile almost sent me to tears, as it was brighter than the sun that shone on us all that day. As the two continued to make their way down the aisle my eyes could not break from the true beauty I was gazing upon.

After a small kiss to her grandfather, her hand was given to mine, and I knew I would protect that hand with my life from that moment forward. From that point on I don't remember anything except being so focused on her that I literally had a tunnel vision of love. I don't honestly remember much except how her face looked as I gazed into her eyes for what seemed like eternity, and I didn't want to leave. I felt, for the first time in my life, at home in a deeper way that I had ever felt. Her heart was my home and I never wanted to leave until the day God took me from this earth. I knew this to the depths of my soul. The ceremony proceeded and at the end we exchanged rings and a kiss that sealed our enduring love. Nothing in my life leading up to this moment held any weight in comparison to the weight I held in the one thing that mattered most to me in this world now, my family. I just want to repeat that because even writing it brings such great positive feelings. MY FAMILY.

The reception was held at a luau where we all partied and drank like nothing else in the world mattered, because that night nothing else in the world did matter. No one knows this, but at one point I went away to get a drink and I just stopped for a moment to look at all the people I loved gathered in attendance to witness me marry the love of my life. I couldn't help but thank God for all these amazing people blessing my life, and this amazing woman I would be able to spend the rest of my life with. If I could live in that moment forever I would.

The next day everyone gathered at the docks to go on a huge snorkeling trip where everyone got to travel out to a nearby island to snorkel together in water so clear it seemed as though we were floating on clouds. It was the perfect ending to a perfect weekend. To this day the image I hold in my head of that day is that of a picture candidly taken of my new wife and me. I was in the back of the boat looking out over the water with both of my hands on the rail, shirtless, wearing yellow swimming trunks. With olive skin and dark brown hair, wearing red bottoms and a white top, was my wife with arms lovingly wrapped around my waist from behind, with her face leaning against my left side. We were embarking on a new journey together in life and we couldn't be happier to have each other on the trip as a partner. We were looking on to our future together. We were at home in each other's hearts, and this moment was the personification of true love. Everything I did in my life from this point forward was for my family, and this meant more to me than any other man could comprehend.

As the week ended we were soon thrust back into the real world and the real world is not the easiest place to live. Upon returning home, the NFL draft was only weeks away, the day that would determine my fate was soon approaching. Leading up to the draft there was silence from all the NFL teams and my agent as the behind-the-scenes preparation was ensuing. Finally the day arrived and a few close friends and family gathered at my apartment in Oregon to watch the draft unfold. I was listed to potentially be draft late in the second day around the 5th-7th round, but nothing is a sure thing.

The first day was Saturday and because I knew I wouldn't be drafted that early, I didn't spend much time focused on the TV. That day a couple of my teammates were drafted in the early rounds and I was so proud to see their dreams come to reality. The second day arrived and I awoke to butterflies that could not be described. These nerves were worse than any game I had played in.

The rounds ticked off little by little as the hours went on. As soon as the fifth round hit my phone rang from a number I hadn't seen before; it was a team calling to talk to me. "Hi, is this Anthony Trucks?"

"Yes" I responded.

"How are you?"

"Good' "Have any other teams called you today?"

"Yes." (I had to say that to make them think I was popular).

"Ok, well I just wanted to check and see how you're doing and let you know we're interested"

Essentially teams were calling to check up on me and see what interest the other teams had in drafting me. I received a few of these calls over the next few minutes, but one team seemed more interested than the others, the Tampa Bay Buccaneers. When they called I was told by the linebacker coach that he really liked my play and that he wanted to draft me, so he was going to go into the room and fight to get me drafted in the 5th round. The fifth round passed and the Buccaneers had drafted someone else.

Next came the 6th round and I received a call from the same coach with the same words being spoken, this time with a little more fervor. The 6th round passed and I still was not drafted. Finally the 7th and final round approached and again I received a call from the familiar voice that had previously promised to fight to get me drafted. He said they had two picks in the 7th and I for sure would be one of them.

The first pick of the 7th round for the Buccaneers passed without my name being called. I was elated because I knew the next pick would be a calling of my name, and I couldn't wait to see my name scroll across the bottom of the ESPN screen for the first time. "And the Buccaneers choose with their final pick of the 7th round.......Justin Phinisee from Oregon," They had drafted my teammate. A feeling of sadness and happiness set in as I was sad to have not been picked, but I was happy that my teammates had been. The draft finished almost 20 minutes later, and within 5 minutes of the draft the buccaneers called to sign me as a priority free agent, which came with a small signing bonus. How could I be mad, although I hadn't been selected I was now a Tampa Bay Buccaneer. My plan for being great was still on pace and I couldn't wait to start this next new journey with my son and new wife supporting me along the way. I was the head of the household and it was now on me to provide, and I would do anything to make sure they were provided for and happy.

I finally gave my parents a call and they were ecstatic to know their son was going to be a Buccaneer. Not to mention that at this same time I started getting mail and phone calls from every person on my mother's side of the family; cousins, aunts, brothers and sisters and more. Talk about people coming out of the woodwork looking for a handout. This was only the beginning of what life had in store for me as the years progressed.

CHAPTER 6:

ONLY THE STRONG

The NFL is a very unique environment that takes a very unique set of personality traits in order to achieve success and be able to stick around longer than a year. It takes an ample amount of confidence, internal gumption, drive, character, grit, determination, and perseverance to attain success. The NFL will eat you up and spit you out on the backside if you aren't careful, which is why it's given the nickname "Not For Long". In short, only the strong can, and will, survive.

After signing with the Buccaneers I was scheduled to attend a mini camp in Florida at their facility with the new draft picks, and other undrafted and/or unsigned free agents hoping to try out to get an opportunity to get invited to training camp in August. The mini-camp would last three days and I couldn't have been more excited to attend. Upon arrival in Tampa I was roomed with my Oregon teammate in a hotel attached to the airport. The next morning we were all to report downstairs in the lobby to await our shuttle and go over to the facility. As soon as I stepped outside the sliding doors, a wave of muggy heat hit me dead in the face. I definitely wasn't in Oregon anymore, and the smug humidity made that very clear. I started to sweat as soon as the outside air touched my skin, and that would be the moment I realized this was a new adventure in the making.

About 40 players from all positions were there and almost no one knew each other. The stress can be overwhelming for some, knowing that at any moment you could be sent home and have to get a real job, making a life in the NFL and enjoying all its fruits so close, yet so far. Any spot on this team must be earned with more work than is even comprehensible. The stress began once we were taken to a room and given a playbook, then walked through every play specifically. You would think scientists were going over the plays with you. My brain as jam packed with more information than it can handle. Then we had to be able to go onto the field and execute as perfectly as possible, because if you can't, you won't have a job. The sense of urgency paired with the fear of making a mistake gets to a point where you can essentially be scared on every single play you take part in.

That was just the first day. You come to realize as the days go on that not only are you practicing so hard that you get physically drained from the heat and humidity, but your brain gets tired from the mental gymnastics of every play. There is no greater fatigue than that of mental and physical fatigue combined where you just want to eat and sleep. After three days of a weird mix of pleasure and pain, I was sent back home to prepare for the upcoming year.

* * *

All teams take part in what's called O.T.A.'s, or off-season team activities. These are short practices where coaches and players spend the offseason going over plays to prepare us mentally and physically for training camp, which takes place in August. Due to the fact that I did not yet graduate from college, I was unable to attend these practices and I had to spend the entire offseason alone watching DVD's of plays that I could barely understand, and training on my own without anyone else. The biggest problem I foresaw was that I had to prepare for the heat and humidity of Tampa Bay, Florida in the elevation and cold of Oregon. This was going to be a daunting task to say the least. I had to run on my own and prepare to be in the absolute best shape of my life. Imagine every single day having to go out to a field alone, set up cones, and run every single rep at full speed without anyone to push you. It was mental anguish at its peak and I had an internal battle to keep pushing on every moment because no one would know if I missed a rep or went half speed.

A quote that I learned in college and lived by at this time was simple yet profound, "The best kind of pride is that which compels a man to do his best even when no one is watching." The task of doing this proved to be a great character building phase of my life yet again. I remember being dead tired halfway through workouts and realizing that I had to keep up with the pace and not miss a single rep, or go over any allotted rest time, otherwise I would be cutting myself short and unable to show up in great shape.

All I had to keep me on track and accountable was a SpongeBob pocket watch I had found in a cereal box that simply counted up to 60 seconds. If the watch said I had to start running in 20 seconds, then I had to run in 20 seconds. It didn't matter how tired I was, I had to run as fast and hard as I could on every single play because I knew one thing; If I didn't prepare correctly, then someone was possibly going to beat me when I showed up in Florida and, just like when I was in high school, I wasn't going to let anyone beat me on any play if I had the say so. I can say to this day with full confidence I never let that pocket watch or myself down at any moment throughout the entire three months I trained. I also was blessed enough to go to a school that owned an environmental chamber that could simulate the heat, humidity, and elevation, so I would run upwards of two hours in 100 degree weather at 80% humidity. Let's just say I put in the work necessary by taking my brain to a level not usually reached by other people in this world.

I arrived to camp in August and I was with the entire team for the second time. There had been one more mini-camp a month prior to this where I got to meet the veterans, but the time was so short I couldn't even establish any sort of positive relationship with them, not that it would matter I would come to find out. When I showed up to training camp this time I had a pure positive and a pure negative to work with. Positive was that I was in the best shape of anyone in camp who had not been around OTA's, according to my strength coach. The negative was that no one knew me or cared about me, so I was reverted back to the world not giving me anything, and in this cutthroat world, they actually wanted to take it from me. This would soon prove to be another great test of what I had harbored inside of me.

Imagine a group of grown men in top physical shape, and angry, fighting against each other with everything they had to secure a job so they could feed their families. The environment was ridiculously hot and humid, so much so that at one practice I lost 12lbs in sweat in two hours, and while walking off the field, each step taken sweat squirted out of the eyelets of my cleats. Now imagine that amount of effort being given in that environment every play of every day. Welcome to NFL training camp. To make matters worse, I was the guy who hadn't been around during offseason so I was an outcast, simply along for the ride. No one liked me, and no one really went out of their way to make me feel accepted. I was third string behind a 10-year starter, and a 2nd round draft pick at my same position.

The special teams coach didn't like me very much. It was hot and humid and I fell back into the mental and physical fatigue I had felt before. My teammate purposely gave me false information on a play and watched me mess it up and to make matters worse, I lost a necklace with a picture of my son engraved on it—I was starting to dislike football more and more each day. After two weeks I started not wanting to eat, not being able to sleep, feeling homesick for the first time due to being away from my son and new wife. The overwhelming feeling of discomfort crept in so much that for the first time in my life I had given up and decided to quit.

I called my agent and told him I was done and he was, for obvious reasons, pissed off. I called my college coaches to see if my scholarship was still in place so I could finish school, and they were taken back. I eventually called my wife and told her it was too much and that all I wanted was to be home in her arms, and she couldn't believe what she was hearing. The thought of how it would feel to be on a plane the next morning headed home became the only thing I could think of to make me happy. My mind was in a very dark place and I just wanted out of this place. I sat at the desk in my room looking myself in the eyes realizing I couldn't handle this distress anymore. I headed downstairs to find my coaches and give them the news that I wanted to quit.

As I went down the elevator all I could think about was going home and how happy I was going to be. I made a left out of the elevator and headed down the hallway. As I rounded the corner I saw that I was about 30-feet from the coaches' room where they were all meeting, and as I approached, the hallway seemed to shrink smaller and smaller. After about four steps something in me told me to stop and I couldn't bring myself to walk any farther. I turned around to find a man named Eric V. who was with the team's player personal, his job was to help players out with whatever they needed. What were the odds of him being right there of all the places? He could have been anywhere in the entire training camp; but he was right there at that very moment when I couldn't bring myself to muster enough strength to continue on with training camp? This couldn't be a coincidence. He took me outside and we sat and talked for a while. He asked me what was going on and I candidly told him how I was feeling about the situation. I filled him in briefly on my past leading up to that point. His advice and perspective was simple yet powerful. He asked me, "How would you want your son to remember you, as the man who got here the way you did, or the man who gave up and left?" That perspective was all I needed to set my sights forward and keep up the grind. Now don't get me wrong I still hated every waking moment of being there for the next two weeks of training camp, but my reason for staying was too great to give up.

I gave my all every day, and it just so happened that the very next day when I went to practice the grounds keeper had found my necklace and placed it on the cork-board at the locker room. If I had left I would have never seen it again, and there is no way that could have been a coincidence; I knew I was supposed to be there. I made it to the last cuts for Tampa Bay that year, even against my belief that I would. After a successful test to my character I was eventually cut and sent home. I knew it was not the last time I would play football, though, because knowing I had endured that situation gave a new belief in my ability to succeed. Not to mention I reflected back on something that I had all but forgotten; what the game of football meant to me. How had I let a game I loved so much become a burden just because it wasn't what it had been all those years? The NFL is a cutthroat business through and through, but it was still an opportunity to make a GREAT living playing a game I LOVE. On flight ride home I wrote a simple quote that I still look to in times of trial. The quote reads:

"*Impossible? Never that. When someone thinks that someone or something is perfect or impossible it cannot be, in the truest sense of the word. The pure fact that nothing and no one is perfect is a testament to this. So no matter how small the possibility, it still exists. Therein lies the possibility that nothing is impossible.*"

I arrived back with my wife and son in Oregon to sit and wait for teams to eventually call me to fly me out and put me through workouts and hopefully get picked up. My wife had graduated and was working on her master's degree at this time, while I came home to enroll in classes and work on finishing my bachelors. For the first seven weeks of being home in Oregon I received no calls and it was looking like my career in the NFL was all but over. I had been training, but as it got deeper into the season I started training less intensely since I didn't see the point of staying in shape if I wasn't going to play.

Then I got my first call. The Seattle Seahawks wanted to fly me up the next Tuesday on week eight of the NFL season, and I was pumped. It was my first NFL team try-out ever and I didn't know what to expect. I packed my bags Sunday night and was on a flight Monday afternoon, arriving that night to get medical screenings completed so I could work out early Tuesday morning. Teams usually fly guys in for workouts on Tuesdays because it's the NFL's players' day off, so if they sign someone they can get him ready for the next week pretty easily. So I completed all the medical aspects and it was time for the workout. Long story short, I was in shitty shape. This wasn't the same player that was working out for the pro day who could go forever without shutting down. I was the only linebacker and after the 40, my legs were spent. I was put through drills and I was in such poor shape that by the end I could literally not move my legs faster than a jogging pace. I looked like trash and I literally threw a golden opportunity to play for the Seahawks out the window because I didn't keep myself in shape to prepare for this exact opportunity. I took this set back as a learning experience and I knew it was time to fix it.

After I flew back home I vowed I would never let something like that happen again. I called my agent and he was obviously a little frustrated, but he didn't give up on me. Every day after class I would walk to a nearby field that had a track and went back to the work ethic that had gotten me to Tampa in the first place. I ran until I couldn't run anymore, lifted like crazy, and I made sure I was prepared as if my life depended on it, because it did. I started to get calls every week, and every week I got better and better. I took trips for workouts to the Texans, Broncos, Lions, Panthers, Bills, and a few others.

The next big workout call would come on week ten from the Washington Redskins. The problem was that the workout interfered with an anatomy class that I was enrolled in that was graded on three tests you would take throughout the quarter. I had already missed the first test so if I missed this second one my entire grade would rest on the grade of the final. I actually told the Redskins that I could not make it out to the workout that week and that I would have to reschedule for the following week, if they would wait. They agreed. I killed the test and prepared to fly out the next week for a workout with a team that seemed to like me enough to wait on me. I flew out and killed the workout, but they didn't ask me to stay, just like all the past teams. The workout started with medical exams, then measurements for weight, a 225lb bench press test, then we went outside to run a forty and do position drills in the snow. I sulked home and prayed that I would get another workout the next week, as it was closing in on the end of the season.

I received no calls on week twelve for a workout and my spirits were dropping. Then week thirteen hit and the phone rang. The Washington Redskins were going to fly me in and sign me. YES!!!

My wife was totally supportive at all times. Without her none of this would have been possible because she was holding us down daily by earning her master's degree and taking care of my son. She was a trooper like none other and I was lucky to have her in my life.

I took a flight to Ashburn, Virginia where the Redskins practice facility was and spent the next three weeks of the season on the practice squad hoping to get pulled up to active, but that didn't happen. Essentially you practice with the team in every aspect imaginable and if someone happens to get hurt, they pull you up to active roster to play in the game. It was a weird feeling there because I literally came in with three weeks left in a sixteen game season and no one knew who I was, or even cared about me being there. The season came to a close and I was on a flight back home to Oregon to watch my amazing wife graduate suma cum laud with her master's degree in special education from the University of Oregon, and I couldn't have been more proud of her. When she finished it was about time for me to report for offseason O.T.A.'s, so we packed up our little family and everything we owned and moved ourselves to Ashburn, Virginia. We filled our champagne 99' Chevy Tahoe to the brim and shipped it over to Virginia. We checked and carried on the maximum amount of bags possible as we headed to our new home. I remember walking through the airport that night with at least eight bags all over my body. Not to mention the flight where we took up every inch of floor and overhead space you could imagine. Then we sat there together with our young one ready to fly across the country together to make a new home and life for ourselves.

We moved into a little two-bedroom apartment with one room for our son and one room for us. The coolest thing happened within about a week of moving in to the apartment, our son Anthony Mack Trucks managed to potty train himself almost overnight. One night he was in diapers, and the next he was using the toilet. I would go to work from 8a.m.-12p.m. and be home with my family for the rest of the day. It was an amazing schedule, allowing us tons of time to just hang together as a family. We took trips with a close friend we had made there and thoroughly enjoyed our time there. The only drawback was that my wife was getting a little stir crazy because she had earned her master's but wasn't able to get a job because she was too busy watching our son while I went to work; a feeling I can definitely understand.

Around this same time we made our first big purchase in April, 2006, which was our first home. It was an amazing feeling to know that throughout my life of never having a truly nice home, I finally was able to afford one of my very own to share with my family. The only problem, which we wouldn't realize until years later, was that we bought a $500,000 home with nothing down right before the huge housing crash. So our home's value plummeted right around the time the next shortfall in life occurred.

Training camp arrived for the Redskins and I had prepared to the best of my ability, like I did with everything in life and football. I learned every play I possibly could so that at practice I could be mentally ahead of the game. I knew all three-linebacker positions as well as all my special team's plays. I could literally go out and play any position on special teams, or linebacker if needed, which made me more valuable as a player. That year we also got a new position coach who was a good guy but in my eyes too young and green to be taking over the entire line-backing core. Our defensive coordinator was a man who years later would be made famous by "bounty gate" which was something I knew nothing about or suspected at the time he was my coach. Training camp, for me, was not as bad as Tampa and I did, in fact, not hate it as much. Yes there were long, hot practices where I couldn't wait to get home to lay in bed. Urine tests in the middle of the night to make we weren't using any P.E.D.'s. There were great battles for positions like every camp has. The difference was that I had been here long enough to establish a relationship with my teammates, which made me feel more accepted than other places I had played. Also, my wife Tanya, who had flown back home while I was in training camp, had flown back in and was staying with a friend in town so whenever I got a break she would come and pick me up and take me out for a little while to relax with her. This great feeling would be short-lived though.

I had a great training camp, in my eyes, and I played very well in all of my pre-season games. One game I actually had a sack and forced fumble on a blitz that resulted in a touchdown for a teammate of mine who recovered the ball; a person who in fact got demolished on the play and luckily got thrown into the path of the ball. The crazy part was that the next day our website touted him as the star for having made the touchdown, when in fact I made the play. It was O.K though because I made number seven of the sports centers top ten plays of the week. I started to garner fans as well.

My dad followed the message boards, and some of the fans that at first didn't know who I was, or care about me, started to become vocal fans saying how much they liked me on the team. After the preseason ended there was a voting section on the Redskins website that listed four names, asking fans to vote for their favorite young player they thought played well enough to make the team. First on the list was the first round draft pick, but second was actually me, and I was elated. I couldn't wait until final cuts to NOT receive the phone call. So on that day my wife and I sat by the phone waiting for what seemed like forever to find out what the verdict would be. If I received a call I was cut, if not, I had made the team. Hours and hours went by and I felt I was in the clear, and then the phone rang.

"Mr. Trucks this is the Redskins. We're going to be releasing you. Then we will be signing you to the practice squad. It was half bad, but there was nothing I could do. I had so badly wanted to make the team, but it wasn't in the cards. In fact I came to realize that the fans were a little taken back by the decision as well.

I got interviewed three times the next day by reporters wondering if I was mad for not making the active roster, to which I responded, "It's not up to me to make that decision, It's up to me to prepare to play so that when I am needed, I can perform for my team." That week was a long one in my heart because I had to prepare again, knowing I wasn't going to play that week. In the first game of the 2007 season, three people got injured, but none were in my position so I knew I wasn't going to be pulled up. It was O.K though because I still had the rest of the season to wait it out.

I had just moved into a new apartment and signed a lease. I purchased new furniture and I was taking my time settling into the home I would live in for the next 3-4 months of the season. I couldn't wait to get suited up and play in my first game so I was just going to keep fighting and working daily to reach that goal.

After that first game we, as a team, had a couple of days off, one of which was Tuesday, which is a day off for the entire NFL. Tuesday is also the day when roster changes are made by 4p.m. EST. That Tuesday my family and I had decided to go out to eat with a buddy of mine, and a team-mate who had been cut from the Redskins the week earli-er and had just been signed with the Niners. We were just hanging out and talking about life and how it was crazy that they released him. In fact his mom happened to work for the unemployment department back in California and he was saying that if anything happened I could reach out to her to get set up for unemployment benefits, to which I responded by telling him I was good and would be here for the year. We all joked about it and that was the end of that conversation. I remember getting up to head to the bath-room and not more than five seconds later my phone rang with a Virginia area code. I picked it up and said hello to which the response was, "Hi Anthony, this is the Redskins and we're going to be letting you go. How soon can you make it down to the facility with your playbook?"

My heart sank. I could not believe what I had just heard. Not more than twenty minutes earlier we were discussing this very thing and I shut it off as if there was no way it could happen. I had just moved into a new apartment, just bought a house, signed a lease, bought furniture, and was all settled in, prepared to earn my spot on the roster sometime during the season, and boom it was all taken from me. I couldn't help but feel identical to the way I felt when I would come home as a child and see the black car parked in front of my house ready to make me move out of a familiar place. I slowly made my way back to the table to break the news and everyone thought I was joking when I first told them.

"Yeah right!" they all said. It took a few minutes for them to realize I wasn't joking then it all set in. To say that dinner was ruined would be an understatement, I wanted to damn near cry. All the hard work and effort over the last year, the moving of my family, and this is how it all played itself out? It sucked horribly.

We got our check and I made my way back home to drop off my family before grabbing my playbook and heading into the facility. I made my way in and was met by the General Manager who had apparently been wait-ing for me. He grabbed my playbook and instructed me to head down to clean out my locker and see the training room staff to get my medical release of good health. It was all so surreal because I seriously did not expect this to happen in any of my mental outcomes. I grabbed my things, signed off medically, and then went upstairs to see if any coaches were around to speak with. I went into the linebacker room and saw my name had already been erased and my backup had been promoted to my position; something that still perplexes me to this day. No position coach was around anywhere. The only coach I found was my special teams coach who was a respectable man. He told me it wasn't anything personal, just a numbers game and that I should stick close to town because they would be calling me back soon. I left with a little hope that was short lived as my close friends and agent clarified that something like that happening is a rarity.

I went home and stared at the walls, feeling like a failure. The only positive was that I was in the arms of my loving and supportive wife who always had my back through the ups and downs. I was providing for my family just fine, but it's tough at any point to find out your jobless and you have a family. So we sold our furniture, packed up our belongings, shipped our vehicle back, said bye to our friends, and made our way home to live in the house we had purchased for the first time.

When we arrived home I started to prepare much like I had done in the past by slaving away at the weights waiting for a workout to come along at any time. My wife applied for and attained a position as an academic advisor at a school for kids with disabilities in a neighboring city called Pittsburg, which isn't a very savory town to speak of, but it was work and it was in line with her master's degree. For the next two months we worked alongside each other as we always had. I had my son during the day when she went to work and I got my workouts in when I could. Since NFL team tryouts were on Tuesdays, they would usually contact you by Sunday notifying you of your summons, then book a flight and fly you out by Monday night. Then they would put you through a workout Tuesday morning. I had multiple tryouts during this time with the Lions, Panthers, Texans, Bills, and a few more. If I didn't receive a call for a workout I would hit the field and weight room on Tuesday as hard as humanly possible so that I would never be out of shape like I was for the Seattle workout.

One fateful Tuesday I had not received any calls for a workout so I went to the weight room and lifted, then hit the field and ran for about four hours until I was spent. I hopped in the shower at about 4p.m. PST and by the time I got out I had missed about eight phone calls. Four were from my agent, two from his partner, and a couple from a number I didn't recognize. The first thing I did was call back my agent, but he wasn't answering. So I called his partner and he filled me in on what was going on.

"Anthony the Pittsburg Steelers want to fly you out to-night for a workout in the morning." to which I responded, "O.K, but I just got done doing a monstrous workout and I am not sure if I will be able to perform at my peak by morning."

His next words were simple yet very strong and effective in their meaning and delivery. "Do you want a Fucking job?!"

"Let's do this," I said. I was out of the house by 5 p.m. and on a flight by 8:30pm to Pennsylvania. I remember this trip so vividly because I was the most worried I had ever been about a workout in my entire life. I knew how it felt to perform poorly from my run in with the Seahawks, and I did not want a repeat of that performance ever again in my life. I wasn't even able to sleep on the plane because of my nerves or even get a good night's rest.

I landed in PA at 6 a.m. EST, which is in fact 3a.m. my time. I was exhausted. I didn't get a chance to eat or sleep and I was basically a tired zombie from the crazy hard workout I had completed without the ability to recover properly. Once I exited the plane I was met by a representative of the Steelers who gave me a quick rundown. They had flown in two guys and we were both going to do a workout. After the workout one of us would be signed, and the other would be sent home without a job. Great, it's not like that helped by adding more pressure to the already defeated mindset I was using in my tired stupor. We drove from the airport into Pittsburgh to pick up the other linebacker who had apparently flown in the night before, and gotten a good night rest. I don't even remember the trip because I was passed out in the back of the car just trying to rest up before the workout.

We pulled up next to a hotel, the driver made a phone
call, and out walked my roommate from Indianapolis who
looked every bit the same as the last time I saw him. Talk
about a moral loss that just about put a nail in the coffin.
He is this guy who was a better numerical athlete than
me on paper at the combine, who got drafted in the fifth
round when I went as a free agent, who is well rested,
and actually showed a small grin of victory when he saw
who his competition was. I was already preparing myself
for the plane trip home in my head. Before that though,
we had to spend the next few hours going to doctors'
offices for medical exams to make sure we were healthy
enough to play.

As we made our stops around town, going from doctor to doctor, I spent every second possible with my eyes
closed, sleeping in chairs when I could find them. By
about 11 a.m. we had finally made our way back to the
Steelers facility that was tucked behind some large medical offices, and right next to a river on the south side
of Pittsburgh. The Steelers facility is actually a mirror
image building where the other half is shared by the
University of Pittsburgh football team. We both walked
in and were greeted by the General Manager and a couple of scouts, one particularly that I remembered from
Oregon years ago in my pro day who said he respected
my work ethic, drive, and determination. He showed us

to the locker room where they had prepared clothes for us to wear during our workout.

It was now time for me to get dressed and take this field. As I sat there getting dressed I thought back to everything I had done in my life and how this very moment could affect my life forever. I was lucky enough in the moment to actually KNOW that this was a defining moment in my life. I was as tired as a person could be as I got ready to take the field—but was I too tired to perform at my best mentally? NO! So as I got dressed I made a promise to myself that I would go out there and give everything I had on every single rep I took, no matter how tired I was inside. I was going to leave everything on that field. I got dressed and at about 11:30 we made our way out to the field.

We warmed up and began our workout. It started with a forty yard dash, then progressed on to agility drills before ending in a multitude of position specific drills that were watched like hawks by the scouts present. I honestly don't even remember how I felt I did throughout the workout, except that I gave every ounce of me I had to make sure I could leave that field and know I had gave it everything I had, so I would have no regrets heading home.

When the workout was complete everyone shook our hands, thanking us for attending then sent us back inside to take a shower and await the decision. To be honest, I was already asleep on that airplane going home in my head. How could they ever decide to keep me over the other player, was beyond my comprehension, seeing as how on paper it was by far the better choice. I hopped in the shower, washed off, and, as I was stepping out of the shower, I was greeted by a scout who said, "Congratulations Anthony, you're now a Pittsburgh Steeler."

I couldn't believe it. In fact I thought he was joking and I started to laugh it off until I realized he was far from joking. "Get yourself dressed because we need to head upstairs and get you all signed up and meet coach Tomlin and the rest of the coaches."

I quickly got dressed and was out of there before the other guy had even turned off his shower. I had attained the goal I set for myself before leaving that locker room by pulling everything I had inside of me out, and leaving it on that field, instead of telling myself I had lost before I had even begun.

I went upstairs and met the coaches for the first time, signed my contract, and was brought back down to the locker room. I was sent to meet the equipment guys who took over while they fitted my shoulder pads and helmet to make sure I had all the right gear. Then he spoke four words that almost made me crap my past. "Practice starts at 1." I turned to face a clock that read 12:20. How in the world was I going to be able to perform at practice when I had barely made it through a non-contact workout for 30 minutes, and Wednesday practices in the NFL are usually two hours, and full pads? So I headed to my locker, got dressed, and walked out onto the field in a sea of faces that were just as surprised to see me as I was to see them.

I literally did not know a soul and I was too tired to even want to say hi to anyone. I honestly do not even remember that first practice, expect for one play. I was playing on the defensive scout team against the starting offense and Big Ben. They snapped the ball, which resulted in me running full speed to my left to meet a big Samoan right guard; heading left full speed in my direction. He outweighed me by 100+lbs easily, and based on what everyone has told me. I laid into him with everything I had and the crack of our pads could have been heard across the field. He drove me out of that hole like a baby trying to stop a herd of elephants. I still wonder to this day how that guy felt when he found out I had beaten him out for the job.

When the practice day ended I was left the facility and headed to a hotel that the team had paid for. They told me they would send me back home that weekend to get clothes and anything I would need to stay the rest of the season. I FINALLY was able to call my wife, who hadn't heard from me all day while I was going through the whole ordeal. She was happy and excited for me and it seemed all was right with the world again. I spent the next eight weeks of the season in Pittsburgh getting to know my teammates, exploring the city, practicing, and just enjoying myself. I felt comfortable with the team and the coaches because they were genuinely great guys, all of them. Coach Mike Tomlin is one of the most class act men I have ever met in my life, and although I didn't get close to him, he left a huge positive impression on me. One of my first memories of him is when he went out of his way one practice to introduce himself and welcome me. Something none of my previous coaches had ever taken the time to do. I told him that I never expected a head coach to do that, to which he responded, "The NFL is hard enough to get into and stay in, so why make it hard to part of my team?" My position coach and defensive coordinator were also very well respected and honorable guys, giving me the feeling of a blue collar work environment where it was easy to play. Both players and coaches knew how much was demanded and expected, so everything else didn't have to be purposefully hard on top of it.

* * *

After the season ended, when we lost to Jacksonville at home in the first week of playoffs in 2007, I went home and settled in, knowing I had a job next season. I was at home for about eight weeks before heading back. I got to spend quality time with my wife and son. My marriage was strong. My wife's career was going well. My family was proud of me. My son was happy and healthy and I loved him more every day. This small bubble of time in my life was the most at peace I could ever honestly remember feeling. All was right in the world for me and I was truly appreciating the success I had been able to accomplish; by trusting my hustle over the years and successfully reaching my goals through hard work and tireless effort.

At that time I re-enrolled in school with the help of my wife. Since I left college early, I hadn't had the chance to graduate. I had less that twelve units left to finish with my degree, and the great part was that I could take them at a local junior college online and they would then transfer them to degree in Oregon. So the whole early off-season from March to June, after returning to Pittsburgh, I was taking calculus classes online to complete my degree in general science, with a focus on biology, anatomy, and human physiology. While all my buddies were out clubbing and partying, I was at home studying. I HAD to graduate and there was nothing going to stand in my way. So I buckled down and focused on everything necessary to complete my work.

Periodically I had to fly home to take tests at the local junior college, I always found it funny that no one in that class full of Asians ever knew that the one black guy dressed in sweats, who actually earned a B+ in the class, happened to just fly in from Pittsburgh the night before and was an NFL player for the Steelers. Just goes to show that you never know who is around you in life.

There is a huge stigma with NFL players that they are all cheaters and womanizers, but in reality that isn't true. Yes, there were many occasions where I would meet one guy's girlfriend on Monday, and his wife and kids on Tuesday, but that wasn't a normal thing like everyone thinks. I, in fact, loved my wife more than words could express, and although I had women follow me home after nights out, I would always turn them away and never so much as even touch them or get their numbers. In my heart I want to be able to be known as a good husband and father; in the eyes of my God, as well as to my family. To me it wasn't worth losing everything I had at home for some random night with a woman I barely knew. Some people would then go on and say, "Yeah, but you were across the entire country so she'd never know," to which I responded, "But, I would know."

You see, there is a quote I found in college that says, " The best kind of pride is that which compels a man do to his best even when no one is watching." To me it didn't matter who knew, because if I knew, I wouldn't be able to look in the mirror each day with respect, and that weight is too much to carry in my heart. So instead of cheating on my wife, I spent time studying for school and getting sickening good at video games. It passed the time and kept my marriage intact and strong. SO much so, that I would call my wife every single morning when I awoke at 6a.m. EST, to say good morning to her, because she just wanted to hear my voice.

During that offseason I was making the biggest strides I had ever made when playing for a team. After the season, coach Tomlin had pulled me into his office and told me that although he didn't know who I was before the scouts signed me on, but he was impressed with how I worked in practice and how I showed up ready to work each day. He was very clear that I had a long road ahead, but he liked that I had a family, because he knew that most guys with families work to support them. It was nice knowing I had the man's positive blessing and respect at that time. I wanted that to carry itself into the next season so as I watched films, practiced in OTA's, hit the weights, and ran every day in the offseason, I was preparing to MAKE this team, this year. I had the opportunity and now all I had to do was take advantage of it.

I actually got really close to some of my teammates, which was cool because for the first time I felt like I was really a part of this team. When the special teams coach called a meeting he made sure to let me know that I needed to be there. To someone who doesn't know the NFL, special teams is sometimes the only way a young guy like myself will ever have a chance to make the team. So to be accepted by the special teams coach is an amazingly positive thing. Things were truly looking up.

Then I had a life-changing scare. One night I got a call around 11p.m. from my wife and all I could hear was my house alarm sounding in the background and the cries of her and my son. I jumped up and starting yelling asking what was going on and if everything was O.K. My heart was in my throat, beating like a racehorse after crossing the finish line and I could barely breathe not knowing what was going on. When I finally heard words I was told what happened. Apparently about five minutes after my wife had set the house alarm, someone tried to kick in our back door by the garage at my home in Antioch. Thankfully the alarm had been set and the siren screamed, deterring the thieves. I can only imagine the fear my wife was gripped with. What if she hadn't set the alarm? Would they have done something horrible to her? Would my family have been safe? It turns out that we knew the person responsible and it happened to be the boyfriend of a co-worker where my wife works. He was a known as a robber and had happened to be in our home for my wife's party a month prior. It was just one of the many reasons that solidify my views of the city of Pittsburg, CA. as not being a very savory town. My wife had thankfully called the cops and they calmed her down, but that incident still shakes my nerves to this day.

OTA's had finished and we had our last minicamp in 2008, and it was now time for everyone to head home for their break during the month of July. During this time in the NFL most guys take vacations and go out of the country to relax and unwind before starting a long and arduous season. I, on the other hand, had a choice between relaxing or finishing my degree, while keeping in shape for the season. I chose the latter. For the entire month of July I spent every weekday on a hectic schedule. I would go to the local junior college weight room and workout before my first 8a.m. class that ran until noon. I would then get over to my second class that ran from noon to two, before my last class that ran from two to four. Next, I would get home and get in my second workout of the day to prepare for double days, and follow that up with a night full of homework and playbook, studying to be prepared for the next morning, and eventually training camp. Let's just say relaxing wasn't a word I would have thrown around at that time. I was on a mission to graduate that summer and that goal was realized on July 25, 2008. I had become the first of my siblings to graduate college, and I did so in a tight timeframe with a lot on my plate. I couldn't have been more pleased and it was just in time, as I had to check into training camp on July 27th in Pennsylvania. I had again proven to myself that I was capable of trusting my hard work on an effort to accomplish a goal I had set for myself.

Training camp for the Pittsburgh Steelers takes place at a college in Latrobe Pennsylvania where we all checked into the dorms. The first day we usually get ourselves familiar with the campus and meeting rooms, locker room, weight room, and then we roll right into our first practices, without skipping a beat from OTA's. This is when the road to a Super Bowl Begins. Every day at training camp feels like ground hog day. You're mentally tired from watching endless hours of silent film in a dark room listening to the same monotone voice yell at everyone for mistakes made. Then there are the play installations where they put in new plays to be used in practice either that day, or the next night. With everything thrown at your so fast, your brain goes on overload. The fatigue is exponentially increased by the physical lack of energy from weight lifting and double day practices in the blaring heat for hours on end. It's as close as I have ever been to a hell on earth where everything hurts and you couldn't sleep enough if you tried. Every muscle aches. You just want to drop dead any time you stop, and it's a battle in practice, taking every ounce of strength you have to give every single practice on every single play. This went on for two weeks and I was for the first time doing well in an NFL training camp.

I had been moved up to 2nd string on special teams in my positions, and I behind guys who were starters on the offense and defense who would most likely never take a snap of special teams in games, so I was in line and on pace to make this team; and I was ready! Then after about a week and a half of hard-paced work, my back started bothering me. I couldn't bend down to tie my shoes without having shortness of breath, so I had to go see a doctor to get an MRI. After the doctor took a look at me it was determined that I had two slightly bulged degenerative discs in my low back, one with a slight tear in it, and sprained inner spinal ligaments. It sounds horrible, but the doctor said it's very common in linebackers; which is equated to about the seriousness of a sprained ankle. With that being said he recommended that I just take a few days off and let it rest and it would be fine. It was a decision I needed to consult with my agent over, because in the NFL when guys get hurt, teams will sometimes wait for them to get back healthy. once they are able to go again they cut them immediately so they can say "Look, he was healthy when we cut him."

In my case, my agent said they really liked me so it would be O.K to take the time off and prepare to play in the first preseason game coming up that weekend. So I took his word and I did just that, rested it. Three days went by; two days before our first game. I had spent all those days meticulously watching film and practice so that when I got back on the field, I wouldn't have missed a beat mentally. The day before the game I went out on the field

206 TRUST YOUR HUSTLE, PT. I

and did the full walk through. I was mentally ready to play and my body felt great going in to the game.

It was now game day and the first time I would get to dawn the yellow and black of the Pittsburgh Steelers on Heinz field, and I couldn't wait. I got suited up and the tingles of knowing I was about to take that field crept up my spine as I tightened up all my equipment preparing to play. I remember running out onto that field for the first time in complete awe of the accomplishments I had made in my life leading up to that point. The only that could have made it better would be to look up into the stands and see my wife and son staring back at me, but they were at home watching on TV.

I was on special teams to begin the game and I remember going down on a punt to tackle DeShaun Jackson, missing him initially, but then getting up and chasing him down from behind to make up for the first miss. I also had a solo kick off tackle. Then it came time to go in as a linebacker for the Pittsburgh Steelers, a feat that so very few human beings ever get. One play after another took place and then one happened that I will never forget. I didn't know its significance on my career until the next morning, but something unexpected happened. I was lined up on the right side of the ball as a Mac (weak side) linebacker. I was in my alignment with a rookie linebacker at my left; the Mike (strong side) linebacker. The Eagles hiked the ball and it was a toss to my left where the running back turned his hips and shoulders, taking off towards the sideline as the quarterback tossed him the ball so he could make a play in the open field against the defense.

When a linebacker reads this, his reaction is to turn and RUN so that he doesn't get blocked by the lineman that is surely coming to block him. Well, this rookie didn't' remember what to do and as he stood there like a deer in headlights to my left, his lineman gobbled him up and started to drive him backwards. As I turned to run, the rookie's right foot jutted back and caught my lead left foot as I tried to bubble around him to try and make a play in the ball. My left foot got caught and I couldn't free it and I went down belly first. As soon as I hit the ground, I went to get up on all fours as fast as I could, then, slam! The lineman that had been assigned to block me jumped on my back with full force. All I felt was my body give out and my left shoulder felt a little twinge pain. I managed to get out from underneath the player and shake everything off. I didn't feel anything out of the ordinary and although I had felt a little twinge on my left shoulder, I didn't notice anything serious, so kept on playing. With my adrenaline high, I probably wouldn't have felt very much anyways. In fact, when my right shoulder was injured in college, it wasn't an immediate pain, so there was no way to know what I would find out until morning when I woke up.

After a game your whole body hurts because you've been running around full speed, throwing it into positions reserved for crash test dummies. It's usually not until the next day that you realize something may hurt a little more than it's supposed to. The next day was the first day off for the entire team and staff in two weeks, so I took full advantage of this time and slept in. When I woke up it was later in the day and everyone in Latrobe was gone, it was essentially a ghost town. It wasn't until I woke up and went to place my laptop on the desk that I noticed I couldn't lift my left arm straightforward without a sharp pain in the rear of my shoulder. I went out to see what time the treatment center opened that day. To my luck, it had already closed for the day and everyone had gone home; I wouldn't be able to see anyone until the following day.

The next day arrived, but the treatment center wasn't set to open until later that afternoon, before practice, but we had meetings to review the game film as a team early in the morning. So I just dealt with the pain, assuming I would go to the treatment center when it opened. The meetings actually went well for me and I got some great praise from my teammates and the special team coach for my play. I was excited to know that my teammates respected my play, and I felt all that much closer to making this team in two weeks. We broke our meeting and were given a few hours to relax before practice that day. I had about an hour to kill so went up to my room to relax for a little while.

As soon as I laid my head down on the pillow to relax, there was a loud knock on my door. My heart sank. See there are only two people that come to your door in training camp; a roommate who has a key and does not need to knock at all, or the general manager who is at the door to cut you from the team. I was speechless and it felt like a mile walking from my bed to the door. I opened the door to see the Steelers general manager, who didn't even say hi. He just said, "We're going to be letting you go today, please get me your playbook and go see the trainers to sign your healthy release form." It. Had. Happened. Again.

I seriously could not believe this was happening again. It was like seeing ten black cars parked outside of my home. I didn't know what to say or do and I just stood there in disbelief for a moment. I knew there was nothing I could say at this point. I simply asked why and he told me I played well but it was a numbers thing; something that all players know to be a lie because legally they'll never tell you the real reason. I told him about my shoulder and that it was hurting and I had been waiting to see the trainers about it, and he just told me to go see the trainers and get it handled.

I slumped down to the treatment center and had the trainer look at my shoulder. After a brief exam he told me that I had two options at that point. I could wait around in a hotel in Pittsburgh and have the doctors there take a look at my shoulder, or I could head home and set up an doctor appointment as soon as I got home. I never signed the release form and I chose the latter. I didn't want to stay in Pennsylvania a minute longer than I had to.

So I walked back to my room, packed up my things, carried them to my truck and loaded everything up, and started the long 45 hour drive across the country back to California. This trip was one of frustration and foundation for me. I was alone in solitude with my thoughts for hours and it was critical therapy for my mind. I had no idea what the future held for me. I knew how much I hated the feeling of constant change, right when I was feeling comfortable. It honestly felt like I was reliving my childhood emotions of being uprooted once I was settled. I needed that time to be quiet with my thoughts and have no other outside insights. It was just the road and I; and I wouldn't have had it any other way.

When I eventually got home, after having been up for so many hours without sleep, I was delirious. I had just about finished a case of 5-hour energy drinks on my trip home just to stay awake and avoid getting a hotel room. I slept in couple of truck rest stops and that was about it. When I got home I was happy to again get to see my beautiful wife and my happy son.

I immediately contacted the head trainer at the Steelers to have him set up my appointment with his doctor and he obliged and did so. I went in to see the orthopedic surgeon the next week who concluded that I had in fact damaged my shoulder. The first course of action was to get an MRI, which showed visible damage to the interior of the shoulder. After physical therapy for weeks didn't fix the problem and get me back healthy for the season, the last choice was made; surgery. There went my season. The doctor made it abundantly clear that this would end my season and any hopes of playing that year; something I was very aware of due to my past injury on my right shoulder. The Steelers were notified and they agreed to pay the bill as they were legally obligated to. The surgery was scheduled and everything was on track. Then the day before the surgery was to take place the Steelers backed out completely from the issue and said they wouldn't pay for it. My agent was livid, as was I, and after a few days of talking to them he managed to get them to stick to their obligation and not only pay for the surgery, but pay me my due salary for the year. I went on to get my shoulder repaired and I received a large sum of money that was a kick-start to the rest of my life. This was enough money that if invested right, would be life changing. There was no telling what positive possibilities laid ahead for me in either pursuing the NFL again, like my heart wanted but was afraid of due to the constant setbacks, or settling down and getting a job or opening a business like I had dreamed about for years. I had always wanted to train athletes with the knowledge I had learned through my degree and playing days. Little did I know that what seemed like the beautiful beginning of the rest of a positive life, it was in fact the beginning of quite possibly the worse years of my life.

CHAPTER 7:

SAY IT ISN'T S<u>O</u>

I had endured a lot at this point in life, but I would soon come to realize that what I had endured wasn't the actual test God had planned for me. It was, in fact, a test preparing me for what battles he would wage in my life in the near future. I had a nice home, money in the bank, nice cars, an education, passion, my health, a happy healthy family, and basically everything the American dream was made of. What could have gone wrong? Well, I would never in a million years guess at what did go wrong. What I do know is that without my previous life experiences, I would not be free or alive to write this book you're reading now. I would not have had the strength or faith in God to endure the ensuing storm. I would be a dead man.

After my surgery I was left with a huge decision to make as a man. What do I do with my life for myself and for my family? My marriage was going well, I had money in the bank, I my son was happy and healthy, and I had a roof over my head. The only problem was that with this shoulder being an issue, I didn't quite know what to do next in my life. No teams were going to be calling any time soon because I was out of commission. One of the hardest things I had to do was decide who I was as a man without the game of football to hang on to. This game that had for so many years provided me a base of self-worth was possibly no longer an option. Everyone knew me as Anthony Trucks the NFL player, so who was I to be without it? Now yes, I had planned this day would come, but not as soon as it did by any means.

I made a tough decision that I must honestly say I wasn't completely sold on, and that was to hang up my jersey and start life at home as a regular non-athlete in this world. Now came the ultimate realization; the work world will gobble you up and spit you out because now it's all on you to do the work and use all the life skills you have gained up to that point, to now become successful in a world that almost seems hell bent on taking you down daily. You see, for me I had known nothing in my life outside of football. I had played since I was young. I had never held a job outside of being a janitor and a paperboy and didn't have any interns outside of the ones I held in the sports training industry while playing, and I didn't know how to put together a real resume. That wasn't in any way going to stop me though. I am not a person who does well with idleness.

. I decided to finish getting my certifications as a trainer and start applying to gyms in the area as a personal trainer. I remember driving around with my wife, going in and handing out my resume to training managers in the area. The funny thing was I ran into my first obstacle because it was hard to get anyone to call me back. I gave my resume to the head trainer at the local gym and I literally never heard back from him, even after I called to follow up. This was turning out to be harder and scarier than I ever thought it could be. I eventually landed a job at the local 24-hour fitness that was at the bottom of a hill behind my house. I was eager to get started and I actually was excited at just the newness of the situation.

I started on a Monday and the week was spent going through training with my manager on how the computer system worked, how to approach potential clients, how to close clients, and essentially everything you would think of when starting up as a trainer at a corporate gym. It wasn't actually that bad until I got to the end of the week and experienced something that would end up making this the final days of my career in the world of a being a corporate gym trainer. My gym manager, and the head trainer at the gym sat me down, where they started to question me on my training knowledge, and the 24-hour fitness ways. The conversation started out with a tone that would be expected in a meeting of this sort; where I would be asked a bunch of questions and they would see if I had the correct answers. It wasn't until the end of the conversation that I came to realize that this wasn't going to be the place for me. What started as a tone of questioning for clarification, soon changed to a tone of learning. I was now teaching my superiors about the training industry and I had only been in it for about a week outside of my playing days. That was the last time I ever set foot inside that gym, I never returned after lunch.

Truth is, I am far from a cocky person, but I do believe that if I am not in a challenging environment. then I will never grow to my potential, I will never be GREAT! So I had to move on and do something that I look back upon as being one of the most defining moments of my life.

All my life I have searched for something that few people thought I would be looking for; a harmonious place to call home, to call my own. I wanted to create something like the world had never seen before. I still had all of this pent up energy and passion inside of me to be great, but I had no idea how to bring it out to the world in a way that fulfilled me. I had always dreamed of opening up my own gym to provide an environment for athletes much like the one I never had growing up. I genuinely care about each and every single person I work with and I couldn't wait to help people in their athletic endeavors. I wanted a place where someone could feel accepted, gain hope, build self-confidence and be around people who cared—as well as become a world-class athlete. I wanted to gift the world with my heart and passion for the sports and fitness industry by creating a training facility that was theirs. I wanted it to be something unlike the world had ever seen before. I wanted to provide a place that paired my experience at the highest level in the world for my sport, with my education. I was blessed to spend time in places other trainers would cut off an arm to an internship for, paired with my knowledge having completed my degree in the area.

My "WHY" was strong, so I figured if I had the opportunity to take the risk and do this, then why not?! So many people live in fear of failure and never take the leaps that can bring them true inner joy. Not to mention that doing anything else literally scared me to death. My wife, far from a risk-taker, was very skeptical and barely supported the idea, but I promised her high levels of success and fast, something that would return to bite me later on. Hindsight tells me that I should have possibly started this path a smarter way, but that's the brain talking. My heart will always agree with my decision because it gave me the ability to test myself, and the inner tools I have to keep on

my path to greatness. Those decisions are what will benefit the world as I share my methods and message.

With the somewhat reluctant support of my wife, I
decided to take a chunk of the money I had and invest it
into my future. I decided I was going to open my very own
training facility. I had never had a gym membership in my
life, I had zero clients, and no business plan. I had literally
no idea what in the world I was doing. What I did have in
healthy doses was my pure optimism and a mindset that
took me three more years to find out about. I knew that I
had been through s lot in my life and have been successful
through ridiculous amounts of hard work, so no matter
what else went wrong, I could trust my work ethic to
pick me up WHEN everything fell apart. So I made the
dumbest decision you can probably make when opening
a gym. I signed a lease for one year for a place that was
8,000 square feet with no plan or idea whatsoever of how
I was going to keep it going. I was so stupidly optimistic
that I thought my simple background in the NFL, my
book smarts, and my passion would carry this business to
unknown heights in a matter of months in what was the
worst economy in America since the great depression. Boy
was that a naïve and stupid thought process. I was almost
doomed from the beginning and didn't even see the signs
that things were going to fall apart. I just wasn't prepared
for how far apart everything would fall.

* * *

It was November, 2008, when I signed a lease to gain entrance into what would be the first location for Trucks Training, a training facility/gym created by me to train athletes to become the best they could be. This was to be my life's work, a way to create something that not only fulfilled my passion in life, but also supported my family. I actually called one of the local guys who also owned a sports training facility and told him I planned on opening this place. He responded in what seemed rude at the time by saying, "If you're good you'll stay." I took this as abrasive at first, but soon came to find over the years that he was in fact giving me great advice, quite possibly the exact advice I would give to someone entering the industry now. I amassed a team of local trainers to help me start this journey and spent almost every waking moment at this new place, preparing it to open in January. I would get up in the morning, skip breakfast, get down to the gym that was only a mile from my home, and work tirelessly painting, setting up equipment, organizing, etc. for three months until it would finally open. Naively I didn't see the strain it was placing on my life every moment of the day. That strain would eventually burst years later.

After months of prep we opened our doors to the world on January 31st 2009. On the business side I wasn't prepared for what was coming down the pipeline for me. I had allowed a few guys to become independent contractors for me from the very beginning and one of them happened to be the most unsavory character a person would want to be associated with, but I didn't know this until later on in our business relationship. The first six months of this business were comprised of me putting in countless hours training new clients, and trying to grow a business with no idea how to. The other trainers were training classes and making all the money while I sat back forking out thousands of dollars in bills and payments, taking nothing home for myself. Since I had been out of the area and disconnected for so long, I was unaware of how hated by the community one of the guys was. He had no degree, no current certification, and an ego that could barely fit into the building, according to him.

After the first three to four months' things started to show up that made me start to question having this person associated with me. I received a text from his girlfriend saying that he had beaten her in the back of the gym and had changed out the carpet because there was blood on it. A friend of mine who lived with him witnessed him beat his own sister in front of the house they were staying in. He started to badmouth my abilities as a trainer, and the list could go on. We ended up having a conversation where I started asking what he knew about the body and the science. He responded, "Why I gotta know that for?" He had to go.

So one day I called this trainer into my office and told him he couldn't be there anymore. He was livid and started cussing me out saying some of the most off-the-wall things imaginable. He told me that without him there would be no Trucks Training—me the guy who fronted $50k of my own money to start it, whose name is on the building, and who ran the place every day. He left and came back the next day with his buddies to get his stuff, which resulted in me calling the cops to escort them all out because they started making threats while I was holding my newborn son. I would later find out that he took advantage of our computer system to get himself paid about $12k more than he should have over the time that he was there. The funny thing is that after he left my facility, and to this day, he goes around town and tells people that all I cared about was money, even though I let countless people train for free to start out, and that he taught me everything I know; the guy who played four years of division one football, earned a degree in the area, and played in the NFL. I honestly wish I had never had this individual in my facility ever. But again I reiterate, everything has a purpose in life, and his purpose was to teach me patience and awareness of those around me.

During this whole time something was brewing at home that I never saw coming. Prior to me coming home from the NFL, my relationship with my wife was rock solid. She couldn't wait for me to come home from across the country, and I couldn't wait to see her and my son. About the time the gym began is when things apparently started to fall out from beneath me, without me even seeing it until it was too late. While building the gym I was away from home a lot, but I was doing so because all I knew was hard work and commitment to what I was doing. I had a family to feed and I needed to make this work as the man of the household, so I dug myself into work out of a sheer unconditional love of my family, and the desire for their happiness. Sadly, that wasn't the view shared by my wife.

I didn't know until later that she was going through a tough time in life and simply wasn't happy. Our sex life diminished, as I would come home late and tired and not be in the mood. Our personal life diminished as she didn't want to come to the gym, so we spent days apart without communicating and she started looking for something to fill the gap of unhappiness. In the beginning of 2009, my wife got pregnant with twins and it seemed she was ecstatic. My first reaction was, "dang, I have to kick this into high gear." So I went to work double time at the age of 25 to start finding a way to support a family of 5; when I had yet to receive a check for my work at all. We were now depleting our savings month after month.

My wife would cry to me about how she wished I would clean the house, do the dishes, help with the trash, spend more time at home like we used to, but those days were behind us and this was now the real world. In hindsight I wish I would have communicated better, but again I wouldn't have learned the lessons I now have learned. After months of this disconnect while she was pregnant and I was at work, a distance between the two of us grew. I had never experienced things were disintegrating until she started pulling away while I simply tried to do right for my family, and build something for our future.

She started hanging out with people from her work, people I didn't know, and started answering her phone less often when I called. It felt funny, but in my heart I knew how much I loved her and she loved me. I knew that once I overcame these obstacles at work, things would improve. I promised her that the business would do so well she wouldn't have to work anymore and I would be able to support us all, words that did not come true.

My beautiful twins, Tatum Ann Trucks and Taurean Diesel Trucks, were born on August 14th 2009 at 12:30a.m. & 1:31a.m. My heart was once again filled with an indescribable joy just looking into the faces of two human beings that were half me, and a true gift from God. During the pregnancy we had a scare that almost resulted in us losing our twins. We went in for an exam and ultra sound and when the nurse was checking my wife she stopped suddenly, a scared look on her face, and she abruptly said that she had to go get the doctor. I kept asking what was going on and she kept saying she had to get the doctor. After what seemed like forever, the doctor came in and went straight to the ultrasound machine and began to check my wife. What he finally told us is that my wife's cervix was prematurely opening and if left alone, would result in an early pregnancy, and our children would not survive. Our hearts sank and tears poured form my emotional wife's face as I tried my best to console her. He said we could put her on bed rest and hope that nothing happens, but that was most likely not going to help. Or we could perform a surgery called a cerclage which meant he would sew shut the cervix until later when they would remove it and induce pregnancy at a predetermined time, or he could accidentally poke the sac and we would lose the children immediately. As a 25 year-old husband I had no clue what to do. The doctor left us and we talked about it as best we could. It was a very scary time for us, and a hard decision to have to make. We eventually called the doctor back in and with heavy hearts opted to perform the cerclage. The surgery was a success and the pregnancy was a success, thank GOD.

So, when I got a chance to see my children I was elated. The birth itself wasn't the easiest either. My daughter came out first and she was happy healthy and an amazing sight for sore eyes. She was pushed out perfectly and I was able to cut her umbilical cord just like I had with my first son. Then came the difficult birth. My son was head down and ready to be pushed out all the way until his sister came out and he decided to go breach. We had waited for hours that evening in hopes Tanya could push both kids out vaginally and avoid the C-section, but once he went breach it was all but inevitable. She tried to push him out but his heart rate slowed and it was deemed unsafe to do so. So after about 30 minutes the decision was made for a C-section. The doctor came in, placed a covering between our faces and her tummy, prepped her, and started the process. I actually have a pretty strong stomach for this stuff, especially after seeing both of my previous children born, but nothing is like watching a C-section. I wasn't supposed to see but I stood up to watch the process. They literally cut open the skin and sliced the skin and muscle with a hot blade that cauterizes the wound as it goes, then BOOM, out comes a baby. What happened next gave me a pit in the bottom of my belly that I can feel now as I think about it.

My son wasn't breathing normally and was rushed out of the room. My wife and I were scared but there was nothing we could do. I sat next to her as they sewed her up and we both waited patiently until we were told it was O.K to see our son. He was placed in a small bed in a separate room where he laid quiet except for the struggling gasps of air he would fight for every second. My wife never saw this part, and I am glad, because it would probably scare her more than me. I cannot only imagine what it feels like to lose a child so soon after birth and my heart goes out to parents who have ever experienced it. I don't know if I would have been able to handle something like that. I now had three beautiful children and a wife who were all depending on me to support them in this world. All that ran through my head at this time was a singular thought; I was now in some way going to have to work even harder to support my family so they would never have to experience the things I had in life.

I was driven even harder to be at work, fighting to make it successful. The problem was that I was in a catch 22. My wife needed me to make more money before we ran out of our savings, and she also wanted me to be home more. I told her then what I would say now, "At 25 I have to work to build up to have that ability like everyone does in life, because there is no more NFL."

I went back to work at the gym almost immediately. The worst part was that it was almost at the exact same time that I had removed the bad trainers from my gym.

So when I had promised that I would be able to work and make enough money for my wife to not work, I was, however, having to work more, and I still wasn't able to make any more money. So I was gone more and still trying to stay afloat. I was working myself to the bone and receiving no pay for it. I was able to get a couple of my close buddies who were former athletes to come in and help me train, and it was a saving grace. I hung on for dear life until about April of the next year when things were starting to go well at work, but falling apart even more at home. I hired two guys to come into the gym and do sales for us so that I could try to spend more time at home. This was because I was needed home now more than ever. My wife was starting to distance herself in ways I had never experienced before. Almost immediately after having our children she went and got her breasts done and starting going out more than I had ever seen her do before.

Tanya went back to work reluctantly, but now had a new group of friends from work that I didn't know, and some were male. She would go out with a group of friends and I was never invited. She started going to clubs and not letting me know where she was going, or when she would be back. When I asked to go she would tell me I was boring, and I would tell her that things she was doing was unbefitting of a married woman with three kids. I couldn't figure out how we had fallen so far apart. She wouldn't take my calls sometimes, she would choose her friends over me, and leave me alone with my kids all night while she went out and partied. There was a time where I had no idea where she was. I got a call one time at 3a.m. saying she had broken down on the way back from San Francisco. So I had to leave my kids alone in the middle of the night to go get her gas. She was a mess, that night, and in life at that time. It was like watching someone relive selfish drunken teenage years with no control of their actions or remorse for doing anything that hurt someone.

I was putting in countless hours at work trying my best to earn a living for my family, doing the only thing I knew how to do, and the only thing I had a passion to do. At the same time I was having trouble at home, the guys I had hired were running my business into the ground. Three months went by and I couldn't even pay the rent. After those three months and my home life literally falling apart before my eyes, I had to fire these two guys and try and salvage my dream. What made it worse was that people in the community who didn't know me started to talk negatively about me as a person, my business, and the reason I was even doing it. I was literally being torn apart by the very community I wanted so genuinely to help.

Then one day I received a letter from the landlord of my gym who forced me into a very tight spot. The letter read that I owed them $16,000 and I would have to pay it in two weeks or they would evict me from the property. Life was barreling down on me at full speed. My marriage was rocky and the only thing positive about it is that my wife had asked me to help her fund and start a business. She needed to put $70k of our money into an account and let it sit for three months without touching it. She also needed time to be able to write out her program plan, which is essentially her business plan. So, I would help her by watching the kids and letting her work. I thought at the time it was actually helping our relationship, but it was in fact giving her something she could later hold over my head. She proceeded to open up this new business around the same time that I was struggling to keep mine afloat. When I told her about what was going on at work she almost flipped her lid. For the first time in our lives she told me that I wasn't good at what I did and that I should just chock the entire thing and get a job to make money, even if I didn't like doing it. She even recommended I just go work for her when her business opened up in three months.

My heart broke for the first time and I was emotionally reverted back to the earliest days of my childhood where I felt stranded and alone. It was not a "we" anymore; she had left me out on an island to do this all alone. I honestly didn't know what to do. I felt unloved, uncared for, ashamed of not being able to support my family, scared to lose my dreams, and I had no idea how to solve this problem. I wanted to give up and throw in the towel on my business right then and there like my wife had said, and find something that just paid the bills, regardless if I liked it. To make matters worse, it was about this time that our mortgage went up and at the current pace we were going to lose our home like so many others. I wanted to go and hide my light somewhere the world would never see it. I didn't want to continue this dream of mine. I went to bed that night with a cloud so dark over my heart that the devil himself wouldn't have felt comfortable in it. My entire world was coming down on top of me. I was defeated and alone in my heart, more than I had ever been in my life. It was physically excruciating.

Then I woke up one day and made a decision. I decided that I was going to make this a defining moment of my own. I had a wife who no longer supported me in my endeavor and who looked at me with disdain because of my apparent failure to uphold my poorly made promises as a young 25 year-old kid trying to be a man in an unknown world. I owed more money than I could muster up to pay off the debts, I had no plan of how to get out of this financial hole, I wasn't even sure that if I got out of this hole I would be successful, and I had only two weeks to save my gym.

I started by reaching out to a consultant, telling him about my current situation, to which he all but laughed at me. He told me he was amazed that I was still in business at all because of how poorly structured my company was. I spoke with a local person who gave me ideas about how to approach the landlord of my gym and what to say to him to see if I could somehow modify my rental terms, and spread the amount over the remainder of the three year lease I had signed. I put the last $4K I had available to me, per a discussion with my wife, into paying this first consultant to tell me how to save my business. I am happy to tell you that somehow against all odds I was able to Trust My Hustle and make it out yet again.

Essentially I was taught how to fully structure my business to run like a business. I was taught how to create business systems that would allow me to market, sell, advertise, run training sessions, and so much more. I was also shown the one magical trick that allowed me to go from making $7k in one month to $21k two months later; and it saved me from bankruptcy. The solution was taking all the hard work and effort I was putting in and focusing it so much smarter. I saved my business and removed one of the burdens lying on my heart for the time being. In fact, one of the gym managers who had not returned my calls when I applied for his job two years earlier, came to me looking for a job or space to rent. I was again making positive progress.

* * *

The next year I would happen upon a program from a man named Todd Durkin who owns a phenomenal gym in San Diego. His methods and heart changed my business and life in unfathomable ways. Not to mention the mastermind group of his that I was accepted to later that year. In fact, he was responsible for me starting this very book you're reading. The men and women involved in his company, along with himself, are some of the best human beings I've met on this planet. The crazy part is that when I went down to his mentorship in San Diego in March, 2010, he pulled me up to speak about my business, and he actually made a comment about what I was experiencing with my marriage. I have a feeling he personally knew the struggle of family and business, which makes sense because everyone who owns a business and has a family experiences it. He said that I had to make some changes quickly, which was what I decided to do when I got home, but it was sadly too late.

The next issue I needed to handle was the issue with my marriage and my family. Nothing else in the world mattered to me more than my family. My kids and my wife are literally my world. The only reason I fought for the gym was so that I could save us from bankruptcy and be able to show my kids that I was not a quitter.

They were my rock to stand upon in my life and without that rock, I would sink to unspeakable depths. In the beginning of 2010 my wife opened up her business, which is a group home in our home. So we rented a home in another part of town and moved out so that we could prepare for the opening of her new business, and get ourselves settled into a new place. We moved everything we had to this new house and her business started. The year of 2010 was hard for me because I experienced some things that no loving, caring husband should ever have to endure. My wife and I fought every moment of every day, she told me she resented me because I wasn't able to make enough money for her not to have to work; even though I could have if we didn't have to own an escalade or a BMW.

She was now the owner of a business that brought in more money than mine, which made her act as though she was better than me. She told me on many occasions that she didn't need me anymore. For the rest of the year of 2010 I battled just to find a friend in my wife again, because my childhood, where I experienced the one woman I wanted love from, who shunned me, was repeating itself all over again, but worse. She all but castrated me for chasing a dream of mine that I so badly wanted for my kids, for my clients and future clients, and for my heart. Instead of actually helping me, she literally cut me off and told me to sink or swim on my own. The woman I had married no longer existed in that person.

By the end of 2010 my wife was spending evening out until as late as 4a.m. She wouldn't answer her phone when I called and would get dropped off just doors down from the house by unknown cars with unknown drivers. She would go to house parties with the kids and get drunk and have her best friend drive her home, She would hang out with people who worked for her that sold drugs, and would lie to me every chance she got about who she was with and what they were doing. I should have dug deeper into this issue but I was more afraid of what I would find than anything else.

The worst was one night when I came home after work around 10p.m. to find her in my house playing dominos with a 22 year-old male employee of hers, we'll call Cyn, who seemed to be closer than normal. This person had gone on a trip with us earlier in the year and I actually helped take care of him when he had gotten too drunk to make it to his room, so I let him stay on my bed. I personally thought he was a scrubby kind of guy and I didn't think he was someone either of us should consider a friend, he was just a short, fat, uneducated sloppy poor-ly-spoken person. He had a daughter the same age as my son and so my wife told me the kids played together a lot.

The odd part was that one night I came home to find them playing dominos on our pool table, she kissed his daughter goodbye on the lips. I couldn't understand why that would have happened and although looking back on it now, I know why. For the next few months I started to notice her talking to him a lot and taking the kids to play a lot whenever I was at work. One day I also came home to have my son tell me that Tanya and Cyn were upstairs together in a room and mommy was crying, an incident that she denied through and through.

Tanya started getting big into softball and apparently Cyn played as well, so they spent even more time together playing on the same team that I was told I couldn't play on. All the signs were there for what was coming next, but my deep pure love for this woman made it impossible for me to see them.

At this point my heart starts to physically hurt and I have tears welling up in my eyes because I am starting to revisit feelings of pain that I have put away for years, with the intentions of never bringing them back up. If you know me personally, you would know how very hard it is for me to cry due to how much I cried in my past, which means it takes immense pain for it to happen. Every part of me doesn't want to write what is about to be written, because what ensued brought me to the depths of wanting to take my own life. As I sit here alone in a room in Sparks,

NV outside of Tahoe, a room I booked to get away and finish this book, I am in fact questioning if it is smart to write this alone while I rummage back into the depths of pain in my heart. Truth is that I have put off writing this for so long because I knew I would feel like this, but I now know it is time to dive back into my, not so distant, past.

Part of my wife's job entailed her to stay over at the group home on overnight shifts because it's a 24-hour care facility. I had never thought anything of it, but right around this time I started to have a sense that something was going on between her and her employee. I had no proof and no true reason to suspect anything, besides what I felt was possibly going on, so I didn't say anything. One night I woke up with a weird gut feeling that something wasn't right. She was away on one of her overnights and something inside of me said I should go over and check up on her. So half asleep, I rolled out of bed and headed downstairs to the car where I proceeded to back out of our driveway, hit one of our vehicles, and smash in the bumper. I made a huge mess and to top it off when I went over to the house, she was there all alone and I had nothing to worry about. To cover my tracks I told everyone that the alarm at my gym had gone off and I was going over to check it out. The next incident is the one that really sent me into a whirlwind of thoughts that something was going on under my nose without my knowledge.

Around December, 2011, my wife and her friends and this guy were all at my house after she had invited them over to hang out. He apparently had been drinking but we didn't know it. We found out when about thirty minutes after he left. My wife received a phone call from him that he had been driving drunk and ran his car off the side of the road into a ditch, next to the freeway on ramp he was trying to enter. That wasn't the odd part. The odd part was that instead of him calling his family, he called my wife. What made it even more suspicious was that she went to his bedside in the middle of the night and spent the entire night with him at the hospital while I called and kept asking why someone else wasn't there to be with him like other friends and family members. I didn't think my wife needed to be there with someone so stupid as to go drinking and driving when he has a daughter at home. Up to this point, for the past year, I had been telling my wife that the people she was hanging around with were not good people. In college we were around driven and successful people who had higher aspirations in life, and she was now content hanging out with people our age who were single, no kids, lived at home with their parents, and thought it was cool to do drugs and act like they were 21 still. I am a firm believe that you are the average of your friends and my wife was a point proven.

This incident sparked in me a suspicion that I could not quell. For the next three months from January to March I had these creeping feelings that left me distant at every part of my life. Business was up and down because I could barely focus. We argued all the time so I was never happy, I actually got used to being unhappy and faked a smile at work for about a year, and it killed me inside. I had a gut feeling something was going on with Tanya, but I never brought it up and I honestly deep down never wanted to believe it to be true. That would truly mean that everything I loved and cared for in the world would be taken from me.

In March, 2011 I had been experiencing indescribable internal anguish at the thoughts that crowded my brain every moment of every waking day. Then came a trip I was set to take to Colorado for my mastermind retreat that I do every year with the Todd Durkin mastermind. I planned to fly back the evening of my wife's birthday, a day early so that I could be there for her day. The day before, she had gone to a party somewhere with all my kids to celebrate her birthday a day early, but I planned something special. My wife absolutely loves massages and I planned to give her an epic one. I teamed up with her best friend to set up a romantic evening. I asked her to buy candles and get a bag of some things together that I needed, so that when I got home I could pick up my wife and take her somewhere special for her birthday to do something memorable.

I couldn't wait to get home and take her to my gym where I had turned on and heated the room and spa, surrounded it with candles, and dimmed the lights; making it ready for her long massage. Something I absolutely knew she would love. When I got home she was on the couch and I asked her to get in the car with me so I could take her somewhere. She reluctantly got in the car and we headed to my gym about three minutes away. When we got there I had her wait in the car so I could go inside and set up the candles and get the massage table prepared with sheets and blankets, because her friend wasn't able to do it. When I was done the room looked like something out of a magazine. The room had the look of a stone grotto with 5 candles lighting up the steam that rose from the spa flowing past a black massage table covered in comfortable sheets and blankets set up inches from the water

When I went out to the car to get her to come in, she said she just wanted to go home because she was tired. I kept telling her that she could come inside and sleep if she actually wanted to. Eventually she came in, which was like dragging teeth, and as I led her back to the room my heart raced with excitement just thinking of her reaction to the room. As we turned the corner she finally saw the room, but her face showed no change in expression from that of boredom and discontent. Her eyes rolled as her shoulders sunk down upon entering the room. She completely did not care. In fact, she again asked if we could go. My heart felt like it fell out of my body and was lodged under her foot. I had been planning this for a week and it was finally here. I had put so much effort into it that for her to have not given it a second look or thought was baffling. I eventually talked her into getting on the table and allowing me to give her a massage, but in about 10 minutes she said she was too cold and too tired. She got up, got dressed, and headed back to the car while I felt like crying while cleaning everything up. Not only did I *think* something was going on, now I *knew* something was going.

* * *

At the end of the month our anniversary had arrived, March 31st. She gifted me with a handgun, a 40 caliber Glock 23 to be exact. I had always wanted a gun, but I wasn't quite sure why I had been given this gift. The gift would come at the most inopportune time I could imagine. It was only a few weeks later in April, 2011, when my world would come crumbling down around me and I would be exposed to a new set of feelings I didn't know existed yet.

Luckily the gun was never used, but there were times when I would say these two people are lucky that I held my composure. I was at work one evening and in walked a professional-looking woman around my age, 27, with a woman's pantsuit on. She may have been Spanish; her hair was cut short and as dark as an olive. She was inquiring about the programs we offered for fitness training, but it was an odd conversation because she was acting a little funny. She finished her questions, got my answers, thanked me, and walked out. About three minutes later I saw her walking up to the door again with someone by her side; a somewhat heavy-set girl with long black hair who also looked Spanish and was dressed less professionally.

When they came in confusion filled me, I didn't quite understand what was going on. The new girl politely asked me if she could speak with me in my office and I agreed. My front desk attendant's version of what happened transpires like this:

She saw me go to the room with a smile on my face, but a little confused. After about five minutes we both emerged and I looked as if I'd seen a ghost, something, she said she had never seen on my face before. I walked to the back of the gym, grabbed my keys, then I walked right past my assistant without saying a word while she repeatedly asked me what was wrong. I left a client in mid-session to get into my car and leave.

What had taken place in my office that day is something I prayed would never happen in my life. Tanya might as well have stabbed me in the heart with a knife because that is what it felt like. I had sat down behind my desk and the girl who wanted to meet with me sat in a chair to my right, no more the five feet from my face. She started by telling me that she happened to be the mother of the child my wife is friends with, along with the child's father—the young man she spends so much time with. The next phrase would rattle me to my soul, and as I begin to write this, my heart is picking up pace and I can see my chest pumping.

"Your wife is having an affair with the father of my child," she said. You could have heard a strand of hair drop in the room and it would have sounded like a drum. My skin went tight and I immediately felt like I was in a movie because there was no way this was real. She went on to tell me that the reason she felt compelled to come to me was because her daughter, who was four years old, had come home to her and told her stories about how she had seen her daddy kissing little Anthony's mommy on the bed at her daddy's house. Her daughter also said that one time she was watching TV on the end of the bed and the two of them were under the covers and the bed was jumping.

I couldn't have been more disgusted and I literally was at a loss for words. I knew it had nothing to do with this woman before me, but I did have one response I remember saying. "I knew it."

I thanked her for coming, got her number just in case I needed it, and she left the office. I grabbed my keys, went straight to my car, started it up and left while calling my wife. She happened to be at a baseball game that I wasn't allowed to go to, with her other guy friends. So I made my way straight to her best friend's house and just about tore her door down.

My blood was pumping in complete fury and anger, and I honestly could not control my emotions for the life of me. The woman, her friend, opened the door and the first thing out of my mouth, at the top of my lungs, was, "How long has she been fucking him?!" Her best friend, who happens to be the godmother of my children, looked me straight in the face and acted as though she had no idea what was going on. I never felt more disrespected by this girl in my life. I had known her as long as I had my wife and she couldn't give me the courtesy of even acknowledging that she knew something about it. I yelled at her some more for obviously lying, then I texted my mother-in-law to tell her what I knew, because I knew her mom wouldn't approve. I wanted her family to know just how imperfect she was, because I was just seeing red and anger.

I went home and paced around the house for hours before my wife eventually got home. I don't know how I made it through the conversation without flying off the handle, but what I do know is something happened that I let happen, and I wish now I never had. She was able to convince me that this girl was crazy and just tried to cause trouble, that they were just friends, and that absolutely nothing was going on between the two of them. Sadly my desire to avoid the reality of this pain allowed me to believe her, because no one wants to believe something like that. So I texted this mother of Cyn's daughter to tell her she was a liar and that I believed my wife, and she needed to stop bothering me at work. To which she replied "You can ask my daughter tomorrow in person."

I agreed without my wife's knowledge and I left the fight on hold. That night I couldn't even sleep, I tossed and turned with a pain and hurt so deep in my heart that I couldn't shake the feeling. I reached out to my best friend the next day and even he didn't know what to do or how to handle it. We had been talking about my dilemma for the months leading up to this, but this was the proof I had been looking for to make sure I wasn't crazy.

The next day I drove out to meet this girl in a parking lot at a nearby bowling alley to listen first hand to what her daughter had to say about what she had experienced. Deep down I prayed that I would not hear this little girl repeat what her mom had told me the day before. My fears were solidified. There stood a pretty little 4 year-old girl who, when simply prompted to tell me what she told mommy, said, "I saw Anthony's mommy kiss my daddy, and when I was watching cartoons they were under the covers and the bed was jumping." There was now no denying this. Not even I could train a child that age to come up with such a bold-faced lie. I even recorded this little girl so that no one could say I was lying.

I slunk back into my car after thanking this girl for her help then drove to a nearby parking lot and cried in my car. I could not believe what was happening. All I ever did was love this woman with every ounce of my soul, by words and by actions, and this was the repayment I got. Was I the perfect husband? NO. Not by anyone's standards, but did I deserve this kind of heartbreak? No one does. After drying my eyes I got up enough courage to drive home to my wife and play her the video. As she watched I could see her face grimace. Then when the video ended I went right back to using words that wouldn't probably be allowed in a biker bar on a Friday night. We went back and forth forever and her defense continued. She swore up and down that this girl was crazy. She had gotten her daughter to lie for her, she said, adding that she and the guy were just friends, and he worked for her, and they played softball together, and that was it.

I still, for some odd reason, wanted to believe her. This is a person that I can say without a shadow of a doubt had every single ounce of my trust. Every single ounce. We actually had a saying in our house that we taught our son; "Trucks' don't lie." So even when staring straight in the face of proof, I allowed this woman, who knew I would trust her, convince me nothing was going on at all, and I bought it hook line and sinker.

The next month was a blur. It seemed like we fought every day about the same things. She would go to work and come home only to belittle the career I had chosen, and me as a man. -She spent hours on her phone texting someone and she just kept telling me it was work-related, but the phone literally never left her side, and my suspicions never subsided. Since the piece of trash worked for her, I told her to tell him that if he wanted to keep his job he would have to talk to me, and explain to me why his ex was accusing him of having an affair with my wife. Something I am sure she failed to even attempt. I told her that I didn't care what was going on, he needed to explain it to me, and until then, she was to have no contact with him outside of work.

Then one day while she was in the shower her phone rang and she had mistakenly left it on our bedside table. I picked it up, it was a text, and it was from him. I don't remember the exact words but they read something along these lines, (please keep in mind that this uneducated person couldn't even spell correctly so I am having to clean up the words to make the legible for you). "How come you don't talk to me no more? How could you go off and tell someone you love them then just all of a sudden disappear from their lives. I can't even sleep in my room anymore or even watch TV. Me and my daughter slept on the couch last night because I couldn't go in there......." And some more I can't exactly remember.

I IMMEDIATELY flew off the handle. "What the Fuck does this even mean? Why is he texting you this? Why can't he go in his room anymore?" I rattled off questions in my red rage like they were bullets out of a machine gun, and I can distinctly remember her response, and even more painful, her face. Her face showed a lack of care, as if it wasn't even a big deal. Her eyes rolled and her expression showed a complete disinterest in my question as she went back to drying herself off, like I had just told her the a random fact about trees. She literally just shrugged it off like it was nothing, which infuriated me even more. I wanted to strangle her right then and there out of frustration, pain, rage, and sorrow all combined. How could this person who knew me deeper than anyone else in the world cause me so much pain purposefully.

Finally she responded saying that he told her he loved her, but she never said it back to him. It was literally too much for me to handle. I threatened to call him to which she didn't fight. So I picked up her phone, dialed, and the phone began to ring as I place it on speaker. I can picture in my head exactly what room I was in looked like when he picked up the phone. I was sitting on my bed facing the door while she was doing her hair carelessly in the bathroom; listening in as if she didn't have a care in the world.

"Yo" he answered.

"Hey, this is Anthony, why did you send my wife that text?"

"What do you mean?" he answered.

"The text I just got on her phone from you," I said.

"Why don't you ask your wife," he exclaimed. My blood started to churn and thoughts of killing this person flooded my brain faster than the fluttering of hummingbird wings. I couldn't control my anger.

"Why don't you tell me since you're the one who sent the text you piece of shit!" I yelled back. "Why couldn't you sleep in your room last night huh?"

To which he again repeated, "Ask your wife!"

So I turned to her and asked her why he couldn't sleep in his room last night? "

"I don't know," she snorted.

"She said she doesn't know, so since you sent it why don't you just tell me."

"Oh, she doesn't know? Then I don't know either," he yelled. This piece of garbage was playing around as if it was some kind of game. This was some low-life wannabe chubby thug who personified loser; a person I honestly would never have employed, even to so much as mop my floors at the gym. His attire screamed ghetto and he was blatantly disrespecting me.

The conversation was going nowhere and I became even more frustrated. I told him to stop texting my wife period, that if he didn't I was going to personally deal with him. That seemed to be the point where she decided to care. She jutted out of the bathroom and told me to just hang up. His response to my threat was taken about as smoothly as you would expect a tough guy wannabe would take it. He got all tough on me and started hurling threats back. Once it got to the point where we couldn't hear each other over the yelling on the phone. I just hung up.

But when I looked, there she was, standing in front of me with a look that was far from the 'not bothered' look of earlier. I asked her again why in the hell he would send her a text like that, and her exact words she said, "Because in his room there are pictures of the staff and her on his wall, and since he misses me that must be the reason."

"How the hell do you know what's in his room?" I yelled.

"Because I went there once with the kids after the park and McDonalds, and he showed me his room" One of the stupidest answers a person could probably give, and I bought it. Like an idiot, I actually bought it. If at this very second you are starting to lose respect for me, after reading about how many times I have bought the lies, believe me, you're not alone. Looking back I don't even respect myself for the lack of strength I showed in this situation because of my deep love for her, but sadly it gets worse.

The next day she had to go see one of her students at the school, where I would find out later is a cesspool and everyone working there was involved in some sort of adultery. , and Cyn still worked there. I actually thought that as my wife she was on my side of this thing, so I told her to ask Cyn why he couldn't go in his room, and to tell him that if he wanted to continue to work for her, he needed to come and see me and apologize for his words and sending the text.

So that morning she went off to work and I called her after I knew she would have had time to talk to him by that point. "He said it was because of the pictures in his room and the memories from hanging out." Looking back, the visible signs that the two of them were actually working against me makes me sick to my stomach, but at the time I actually believed it. "What did he say when you told him he needed to come talk to me or he would lose his job?"

"I forgot to tell him," she said. I was pissed and told her she needed to tell him ASAP or I would go and find him myself. She agreed she would tell him at their softball game that night. Yes, they were even still playing softball together. In fact, early in the summer the year before, she had an overnight tournament about two hours away with him and her team. I surprised her by driving out with the kids to hangout. Oddly enough, when I showed up she was angry that I came, instead of happy that I was supporting her. Something I understand now in hindsight

. That night after her game I asked her what he said when she talked to him. "I can't make him do anything like that, he's just an employee."

To which I responded, If that's all he is, then why have you been to his house and why do you play softball with him?" She was fighting tooth and nail to keep me from talking to this guy I told her that until he came to talk to me, didn't want her talking to him at all. He can go to work, I said, but that is about it, no more contact.

It couldn't have been more than two weeks later that I found another text conversation when I found her phone unattended. In this text he reached out and simply said that it was hard not talking to her and that he missed her. If that wasn't enough to anger me the next response was, "I know shit's hard. I miss you too."

Yet AGAIN I flew off the handle trying to figure out why in the hell they were still communicating, after her saying how it was hard to not talk to this guy who wasn't even her husband. I was livid and began digging to find out what was going on. Next, I looked up our phone records. As I dug deeper and deeper I started to find more and more heartbreaking information. My wife is a night owl and I would regularly go to bed way before her 2 or

3a.m. bedtime. I never knew or questioned what she was doing at that time, because she had always done it. As I looked back through the records I found night after night where hours were spent calling the same number; his number. Even on my birthday, when I couldn't reach her, I saw that she had talked to him almost the entire time that I was out with my buddies.

That night I decided that I had had enough. I packed up a bag and left to go stay at my best friend's house in Walnut Creek. She honestly didn't even care at the time, as I remember. She just thought I was overreacting because they were just friends. Her response as to why she said she missed him was because they were such close friends, and she was always there for him when he needed help with his ex.

I was tired of this back and forth, and we were getting nowhere, so I decided I wanted to go see a counselor. We went to see a woman in Antioch and although at first it seemed like it was getting somewhere, in the end it was a complete waste of time. Tanya's heart definitely was not into it. I couldn't figure out for the life of me why I was the one putting in so much effort to try and fix this marriage. The person who was having a wrongful relationship, who had three beautiful kids and a loving caring husband at home, couldn't put forth the effort to keep the family together. Selfish would be a grave understatement for how she was acting at that point.

The therapy wasn't working, to say the least, and although we were living in the same house, we weren't living a life together. She would tell me she resented me, and that she wasn't happy with her life. She said she felt as though she missed out on her party years by having a child so young, so she wanted to live it up, even after I told her that people who are partying want what she has. During this time there was supposed to be no more contact with him, but I was still pissed that she hadn't made him come talk to me about this yet.

Cyn was still working for her and I had this gut feeling that he was still in the picture; and the root cause of why I couldn't get her to commit to any form of counseling. I found this to be true when one night they both had a championship city league softball game to play, so she made me leave so there wouldn't be a problem. She asked her very own husband to leave so *he* could be there in peace. So, in my rage I found out when he would be working at her group home again, my old home. After finding out, one morning I told her I was going to wait for him to get to work and confront him at the house. Before she could say anything I was gone. I loaded myself up into my black Chrysler 300 and drove over to wait in front of my former house, the group home. What no one knows is that I had brought along a lighter to use as a fist pack, because at this point I was done trying to use my words.

The first thing I was going to do the second I saw him was to lay into his face with everything my body had. Luckily for him, my wife had cared more about him than she did about my feelings. She called him and warned him not to go in to work that morning, and to call in to work late, because I had to head out to the city with her and the kids to visit her family that morning and we couldn't be late . . . I wasn't done trying to talk to him though.

The next week I found out that she would be playing in another softball game with him, so this was going to be the time I went to find him. Now although I wanted to physically destroy this person, I am a man of faith. While going through these times, I spent a lot of time going to church alone, or with my kids, just so I could keep my emotions under control. But when the day came on the field, it was time for me to go out there and talk to him. My wife actually helped organize this and I think she did so because she knew it was an open area and that I wouldn't do anything out in the open. In reflection, she wanted nothing to do with this plan, but she knew I wasn't going to stop until I talked to him.

I drove to where the game was being help and parked my car then went to where she was waiting for me. The look on her face was of disgust and it was very clear that she wanted nothing to do with this. I would clearly understand why she was acting that way. She directed me to where he was and I headed in the direction. As I approached his fat body from behind, it took everything I had in me to not kick him in the face. He was lying on a blanket on the ground with some guys around him. As I got closer I spoke his name and told him to follow me. He got up and walked the 30 feet to the bleachers behind one of the home plates. No one was sitting within earshot of our conversation. I started, and continued the conversation in a calm tone against all my inner desires to start yelling at him out in the open. Mind you, at this point I have no real idea of what has been going on behind my back.

"Look, I don't know what has been going on between you and my wife but it needs to end. I have known you for two years, you've taken trips with me, you've been in my home, and although we don't know each other very well, we do know each other."

"Yeah" was his response.

I continued on, "My family means more to me than you will ever comprehend. I went through a lot as a kid and because of that, my family is my world. So no matter what's going on between you two, I don't care or want to know; I just know it needs to stop." He didn't respond for a second as he contemplated his answer, then he spoke.

"My bad man, you're right blood. My parents raised me better than to interfere with another man's family." I don't

remember the next parts of the conversation, but I actu-
ally shook the boy's hand and we went our separate ways.
Little did I know that I had just been had by both of them.
She set me up, and he knocked me down.

By this time I was losing some of my suspicions about
what was going on between them. I would, however,
check her phone and phone records periodically to make
sure they weren't talking anymore. Where there's a will
there's a way, though. We happened to be linked to the
same iTunes account so I got receipts for all the apps purchased on the account, and I could see on GPS where all
the phones on the account were located. One day I was
checking my receipts on iTunes and I found an app purchased called *text now* that I hadn't downloaded, so I asked
her what it was. She said she had used it to prank text one
of her friends when she was with her best friend. I didn't
make anything of it at the time, but I also downloaded it
to see what it was and I found out it was an app where you
could in fact text someone.

It didn't hit me just then, but that wasn't its only use
for her. One day in June 2011, I was sitting at home and I
received a text from a number I hadn't seen in months. It
was the Cyn's child's mother; the ex-girlfriend of the guy
my wife had been seeing. She sent me a picture of my car
parked outside of his house at that very moment. Then she
sent a text saying that she saw my wife peeking through

the window. So I immediately went to the computer and logged into my iTunes and went to the GPS locator and loaded up the live locations of all the devices on my account. My iPad was at home, my phone was at home, but her phone happened to be at a house that I was unfamiliar with, but I remembered the area. It was his house. The dot showing her iPhone was literally on his house, which meant that she was in his home.

I called her, calmly for once, and simply asked where she was. "I'm at Mi Pueblo," she answered. That is a Mexican grocery store about four blocks away.

"Is that right?" I asked.

"Yes why" she responded.

"Because I'm on the GPS, and its showing you at his house." The phone went silent for a moment. "No I'm not. That thing is off sometimes." Literally, as I was talking to her, I saw the GPS location dot moving down the street.

"Is that right? It's never done that before, it's usually pretty accurate, why don't you just admit you are at his house?"

"But I'm not," she insisted. Now the dot was actually moving down the street as she had apparently gotten in the car and started driving away. I told her that I had received a picture that showed her car parked out in front of his house. She said "I'm driving, I'll talk to you when I get home," then she hung up.

I could feel the anger climbing up inside me with every passing second as she made her way home. I couldn't wait to hear this explanation. She walked in the door and I tried to be calm and give her the benefit of the doubt, or at least hear her story. She said she was up the street from his house at another employee's house. She just parked her car there because there wasn't any parking. I could not believe the horrible lie she decided to go with. I started a verbal assault that entailed me calling her names I would never have called her in my wildest dreams. I didn't know what else to do. I was at my wits end with the whole thing and she was intentionally doing this. I could not figure out how I had done anything so horrible to deserve this treatment from the person I had closest to my heart.

I left and stormed out of the house again to sleep at my best friend's house; I just could not deal with it anymore. The very next day I went home and as we started talking about the situation, my neighbor happened to walk over and tell us that she saw someone creeping around our house at midnight the night before. I assumed it was a mistake and it was probably just another would-be burglar. But months later my wife told me that it was him lurking around my house, trying to get in, knowing that I had slept somewhere else that night, because she apparently had told him. At least she didn't let him in. Sadly, at this point, that's was a positive thing.

My heart was already broken and I couldn't honestly tell you how I was keeping it all together. Even after talking to this low life and shaking his hand, while she made a mockery of me, she had no intention whatsoever of stopping. This whole year the two of us had been leading up to a trip to Hawaii with our oldest son. We had booked it for July and in all honesty this was probably going to be our last shot at trying to do something to rekindle there was left of our marriage. She herself even said that she planned on making this trip one that would put us back on track. So, as the trip approached, I was getting excited for obvious reasons.

On the other hand, she didn't seem to carry the same enthusiasm. In fact, due to the fact that she had city league softball games, which can easily be missed, she changed her flight and would fly out one day after my son and I. And she would go back one day earlier. I fought it as hard as I could, but she even went as far as to say that I didn't care about what was important to her, because I didn't support the importance of her softball game. I just couldn't fathom how someone would choose playing a one hour city league softball game over a vacation to Hawaii. It just didn't add up.

Regardless, my son and I headed out and got settled into the place where we were staying. We had a blast, just the two of us alone, walking around town and enjoying the sights. The sky was clear blue and the water was perfect. We even took a boat ride together, seeing the crystal clear water that glistened like a wavy topaz mirror, and seeing all the beautiful rainbow colored salt-water fish in the ocean.

The next day came and we couldn't wait to pick up my wife, and his mom from the airport. When we picked her up at the airport, she actually seemed a little more excited to be there than when I had left her. In all honesty, the first day was going well. We went back to the hotel room, relaxed that night and got some food. The next day we went to the beach, ate at a nice restaurant across the water, laid out in the sun, and I played in the water with my son. It was an all-around good day. The next day started out the same, but finished worse than I could ever had expected.

We went out on a boat to go snorkeling, which was a great time, but the entire trip I couldn't help but notice Tanya couldn't put her phone down. In fact, she was texting almost every free second she had. When I asked her what she was doing, she would get really defensive and tell me that I was overreacting. She said she hadn't been on the phone all that much.

When we got back to town after our boat trip we continued having a good time, walking around town and looking at all of the shops. We stopped by a tattoo shop to check out their work, because I wanted to get my twins names tattooed down the sides of my ribs. We kept walking around and in another store we looked at watches. She was looking up something on my phone, so she gave me her phone to look up the price of the same watches online. So I was looking up the watches on her phone and found the same ones cheaper so we decided not to buy them at that shop. We were right next door to a P.F. Chang's and, since we were all a little hungry, we put our names on the waitlist. The wait was going to be another 45 minutes so I figured that since we had so much time to kill, I would walk back over to the tattoo shop and make an appointment to get a tattoo the next day.

I started to walk away and realized I still had her phone, and she still had mine. When I told her I was just going to keep her phone and she could keep mine, she blurted, "Oh, I need it." I knew something was wrong by the nervous attempt she made to get the phone back paired with the shakiness of her voice. When we switched phones she didn't even make any eye contact with me. So I grabbed my phone and walked away.

I started to walk towards the tattoo shop and got about 50 feet away before I doubled back around the backside of the buildings nearby gold pillar. As I approached her she saw me and I saw her fingers motion to quickly close an app on her iPhone. I knew something was out of whack now. I made up a reason for coming back and then headed out again. This time I was planning to double back to take her phone and see what she was protecting. As I came around again she didn't even notice me. She had her head buried into the phone again, so I reached in and grabbed hold of the phone.

Her face was stark with an element of fear before turning pale. I knew I had to see what was on the phone. As I grabbed at the phone, she held onto it for dear life. I had to literally pin her body back against the wall and pry the phone from her hands. Once the phone was free, I turned to take off. She grabbed at me so hard that she in fact ripped my shirt at the sleeve. There I was, storming away from her and my son, yelling at Tanya, at the top of my lungs to, "stay with Anthony!" I hurried my pace and started fiddling with the phone while I tried to see what was on it.

I opened up the recent apps tab and noticed a familiar app called text now. I opened it up to see something that would shatter my heart into a million pieces. The text now app hadn't been used to prank friends, it was her loophole way of texting him the entire time. As my eyes welled up with tears and my heart no longer felt like it was present in my body. I continued to read the exchanges. By this time she had followed me for a block and a half, still fighting to get the phone back from me before I could fully read her texts back and forth with him. As she was still frantically chasing me and fighting to get the phone a man rushed up to us to tell us that his wife was with our son that Tanya had left to follow me. Tanya was so afraid of me seeing what was on this phone that she left our young son alone on a bench in front of a restaurant; in Hawaii. This man coming to tell us his wife was with Anthony was finally enough of a coercion for Tanya to leave me and go get our son.

What I would go on to read was my worst nightmare. The texts read:

"Hey maami, whats good?"

"Nothing Papi, just out here in Hawaii, and I got you a little something."

"What did you get me?"

"It's a surprise."

"Ahh, well that's cool because now I'll have something else to look forward to than you coming back and us getting in because all I can think about is fucking you so hard sideways."

"You better calm down papi before you get all hard and have to beat your shit"

This was my WIFE...WIFE.... and this was how I had to find out what was really going on! On a vacation in Hawaii with my son, during a trip that, by her account, was supposed to help bring us closer. She had made a fool out of me and destroyed my heart. I was broken.

I had to respond to the text "Hey, this is Anthony now. You can have her." It was a text met with no response. I took pictures of the screen and sent them to myself for proof, and I even sent them to her mom. See, leading up to this I had tried everything to get this to stop. I had put up with it, confronted it, forgave it, and I even told everyone in her family in hopes they could talk some sense into her. I even tried her best friend, but she was dead set on taking my wife's side in everything. She never admitted any fault in supporting my wife to go out night after night partying. Everything was a loss, and nothing apparently was going to be able to make this stop.

I cried alone all the way to the hotel, then sat in the lobby and waited for Tanya to return with my son. She finally arrived and I dried up my tears when my son asked what was wrong. My response to him should never be spoken to a child his, but I was in the heat of intense emotion and it slid out. "Your mom has been Fucking Cyn. She doesn't love me anymore and she has been kissing and being with him. She doesn't love our family."

My son started to cry and at the time I didn't care. I feel horrible now, because if I was unable to handle that kind of pain at my age of 27, how was a child expected to handle it? We went up the elevator to our room; I unlocked the door, let my son in first, and slammed the door behind me so she couldn't make it in the room. There was no way I was going to let that person into the room with us.

She immediately started banging at the door pleading

for me to let her in. She had no phone, no key, and nowhere to sleep. GOOD. Over the next hour we would talk through the door and I pleaded with her to tell me why. Why did you do this? How could you have slept with him? To which she responded, "I didn't sleep with him, we were planning to, all I ever did was go on his bed and we kissed.

By this time I was not letting her lie to me about it. "What 27 year-old woman goes in another man's bed and kisses him without anything else going on? And who in their right mind at that age plans out something like that? You're not a teenager in high school!!" As apparent as it was that she had engaged in sexual relations with that boy, she stood true to her guns and lied to me the entire time, saying they never had sex at all. She didn't budge even once. So she slept outside the entire night, and I could care less. It wasn't until the next morning around 8 that she entered the room, after the front desk opened back up and gave her a key since her name was on the room. I gave her the phone back and I took my son and left. What she didn't know was that night I had taken the pictures of her conversation with Cyn and posted them on my Facebook for the world to see their disgusting deeds.

I took my son to a water park nearby while I called my Aunt Anne and uncle who had been voices of reason throughout the ordeal. They had gone through a rough divorce and could foresee what was coming. I filled my aunt in on what happened and oddly enough, I was still trying to deny the fact that she had actually had sex with the man. To which my aunt replied, "Ant. Honey. I am a woman and, based on what you're telling me, you need to accept the fact that she has in fact slept with him." My heart sank again. How much more of this could I put up with before I completely fell apart? I got on the phone with my uncle, who is a very straightforward guy, and he told me to leave her, fight for the kids, and move on. Advice that I really wish I would have taken and put into action right then and there.

I spent what felt like a week, but was only actually a couple of hours, at the water park with my son trying to muster up a smile for him, but my mind wasn't even functioning. My heart had never ever felt so much pain, and I could not figure out why this was happening to me of all people. Most of the time it's the guy looking to do these things, one who is heatless and uncaring, who doesn't fight for the family, yet I was in the opposite position. It wasn't like I was an ugly, low life, loser, with nothing to show for myself. I was a strong caring former professional football player who was enduring this pain because of how much a family meant to me because of my upbringing. I was being weakened and taken advantage of by my only Kryptonite, love.

I finished the day and started the long drive back to the hotel to face the music. I am sure she had by now found out that I had posted the pictures of her texts on Facebook. One thing about her; she has a huge issue with peoples' perception of her. So after trying everything in my mind to get her to stop her affair, the only thing left to do in my mind was to show the world the true person she had become. Maybe she would be too ashamed to continue doing it. Was it a good thing to do? I will never know, part of me would say no because it's best to keep issues like that private in a relationship, but it had been done and it served its purpose.

When I returned I could see from the look on her face that she was mortified about me posting her business on the Internet, and I understood that. My defense was that I had put up with it for three months, knowing part of it, and years prior, when she decided to keep pushing me away and showing me how little she cared about me. Even to the extent of placing that boy above me. I had no choice but to take drastic action. I didn't even want to take down the Facebook picture posts, but her family reached out to me and pleaded with me to do so, so I did. Truth is, people get killed in this world over less than what we were going through There are men and women in prison right now for killing their spouse, or spouse's lovers, for LESS. Not to mention that the gun I was gifted was, on a few occasions, loaded and ready to go out and find this guy in the not so distant future. So in comparison, what I did wasn't the end of the world.

The next days were a blur of fights, yelling, and her eventual early departure back to the states to play softball, with a team full of people who, in the past, had looked me in my face, smiled, and shook my hand knowing what she was doing. She left a Hawaii vacation early to play softball with her friends. I was dreading the return probably more than her because I now had to deal with something far outside my comfort level. I had no idea what was going on in my life now. I couldn't go to work, but I had to, so I went there every day with a heart devoid of any happiness whatsoever. I had to produce fake positive emotions and I cannot, to this day, even tell you where it came from. My job as a trainer is to make other people happy, but I had no smiles in me.

At home all hell broke loose. She had made it home before me, so when I arrived she was on our bed just sitting there with a blank stare on her face. She was more saddened by the fact that everyone now knew, than she was at the fact that she had done it. She even continued denying that she ever had sex with him. It was something I wanted to believe, but just couldn't. I couldn't believe I was, in fact, even having the conversation. I fell into a dazed state that lasted for weeks, but when it ended it would be very bad.

I reached out to my aunt and uncle who were Christians and did their best to talk to us and try to help, but she wasn't having it. She was so pissed at me for posting the pictures that she wasn't going to listen to anyone in regards to fixing the marriage. After a couple of days, following my leaving again to go stay at my best friend's house, she reached out to me and started to apologize for what she did. But, she was still blaming me for being the cause of all she was doing, and in fact she tried to say I somehow deserved it. Her perspective is one that I comprehend, but do not agree with. In her eyes, when I got home I completely neglected her and the family. I was too focused on my business and never made time for her like I had before. She wanted me to just sit at home with her and spend time and not worry about the money. She essentially said I selfishly chose the business over my family, because I just wanted to do it for myself, and that I made false promises that I knew I couldn't keep. The sad part was that her perspective was all off, and that is what led to the craziness. To date she has actually apologized for making those assumptions and has told me they were all just excuses to cover up the fact that she was feeling overwhelmed with life. She said she was curious since she had been with me for so long, and that it was just a crazy time in her life that she wishes she could take back. But this story gets worse before it gets any better. My perspective on the exact same issues in our relationship, with the same things happening, is different.

I was a naïve 25-year old trying to find a way to take care of my family, doing something I not only loved to do, but knew how to do. It scared the heck out of me to do anything else because I didn't know if I could succeed at it enough to feed my family. So when I was not around, it wasn't because I was hanging with buddies, out with other women, or doing any drugs, I was, in fact, at the gym working myself to the bone for my family. I was essentially being neglectful of my family by trying to do right by my family. I just wish she would have come down to the gym, a mile away, more often to see that, but she rarely ever came in. Regardless of who is right or wrong, since there is no right or wrong, my gym was a cause of turmoil in my marriage that was a catalyst to its ending. The thing that was hardest was thinking about the fact that in reality any other job would also have kept me away from home; even more if I had to commute to work and back.

In my eyes it was most difficult because the transition from high school, college, and the NFL where I always had free time due to the type of job I had, to the new "real" world life where I had to be away from home for longer periods of time. So the change from one life dynamic to another, paired with her feelings of being overwhelmed with the responsibilities of life, left her looking for an escape, and she had found one.

One morning, while staying at my friend's house, she asked me to come over, and I laid into her. I told her it had to be over with him 100% if she didn't want me to leave her. She agreed and I forced her to call and tell him with me on speakerphone so I could hear it with my own ears. We went downstairs to our dining room and sat on the sofa together while she made the call. The phone was dialed, it rang, and he picked up.

Him: "Wassup blood?"
Tanya "It's over." A fit of tears left her barely able to
    breathe or talk
Cyn: "Is that what you want?"
Tanya: "Yes, it's over."
Cyn: "Whatever blood, I guess that how it's gonna be huh?"
Tanya: "Yes, and you can't work for me anymore."
Cyn: "Hell no, now you fuckin with my money? You two are
    somethin else."
Tanya: "It's over." She was trying hard to keep her composure.

Then I hung up the phone. I couldn't for the life of me figure why it was so hard for her to break it off with him if she loved me. It made me sick to my stomach that she could actually produce any kind of tears over that conversation. I would come to find it was because she didn't

272   TRUST YOUR HUSTLE, PT. I

actually want it to end that way, something that still sits in the pit of my gut today when I think back to it. I left immediately and went in to work.

Later that day while I was at work simply trying to keep it together, training a group of three baseball players, I remember looking over at the doorway about 40 feet away and seeing a silhouette of a person. I don't have that great of vision so I had to actually walk closer to the door to see who it was. To my astonishment it was the short, fat, scrubby piece of trash with his disgusting long hair in ponytails; in the flesh. I was amazed that he had the audacity to actually show up at my place of business. Never in my life have I had to contain myself the way I had to contain myself at that very moment. Every single part of me wanted to literally kill him where he stood. I wanted to send my fists flying through his face until his blood covered my body. I was that furious. The only reason I did not try to take his life at that very moment was because I actually had my daughter with me and I had a gym full of clients. It would have ruined my career for them to see me beating someone up in my gym doorway. As I approached him, he backed out of the doorway, I followed, and I stared him directly in his eyes.

"What the fuck are you doing here?" I asked.

"I figured I would come talk to you, because she's got us both twisted blood."

"I don't understand. What makes you think it was smart to come to my work! Do you know what I want to do to you right now?!"

He took a step back and looked at me a little funny because he knew what I meant.

"I sat down next to you and told you how much my family meant to me and WHY, but you STILL pursued my wife, MY WIFE! What makes you think I'm going to believe anything you have to say?"

"Look," he began sheepishly, "she keeps calling me telling me she wants to be with me and asking that if she leaves you, will I be with her." I avoided the statement altogether because I had other questions I wanted answered.

"Did you ever have sex with my wife?" Every part of me wanted the words to magically fly back into my mouth because I realized as soon as I said them that I didn't want the real answer.

"Yes." I couldn't believe what I had just heard. The combination of emotions in my body at that time cannot be described with any combination of words that will give it proper justice. I felt anger, fury, pain, and my blood turned as cold as ice. My wife, whom I had let closer to me than any person in this world, that held the only key to my pride as a man being diminished any further, had thrown my pride away and given it to this low life. She ripped my heart out of my body with a dull knife, crushed it in her bare hands, threw it on the ground and stomped on it before lighting it on fire to watch it burn, before peeing on its ashes. My dazed fog deepened as I tried to wrap my mind around this feeling. Although I was having these feelings on the inside, my outward appearance to him did not change.

"You make me sick. What kind of person does that? She's my WIFE! But you know what, you can have her." And with that I turned around and walked in before he could say another word. I was proud of myself for not killing him where he stood. Somehow I was able to gather myself for the rest of the hour at the gym before heading back home to confront my wife about what he had just told me. As soon as I got home and walked through the door I headed straight upstairs and opened the door to find her lying on our bed with the sheets pulled up to her neck, showing only her face with eyes red from crying.

"You had sex with him!!" I shouted.

With a blank stare on her face she said, "I didn't want you to find out like this, I wanted to tell you."

"You had every chance to tell me but instead I have to find out from him coming to my work!! Did you know that he came to my work?"

"No, but he left here angry so I guess that would make sense."

"WHAT??!! Why the fuck was he here in the first place?!"

"After I told him he was fired he went to the group home looking for me I wasn't there so he came here pounding on the door wanting to get answers."

"For what? You already told him it was over, he doesn't deserve any answers."

"I didn't ask him to come by, he's in love with me, that's why he went to you to tell you the truth, so that you would leave me and he could have me."

"Well, he did right because I'm done with you. How could you do this to me? How could you lie to me like this? I loved you more than anyone could ever love someone and this is my repayment?"

"I'm sorry" she cried, as she sat up and started to show life for the first time in the conversation.

"How many times?"

"Six," she answered.

My heart sank.

"Six?" I knew it was lie to protect me.

"When?" I wanted to know everything, no matter how much it hurt.

"My birthday, during therapy the first time, and a few times when I would go to his house while you were at work and his roommates would watch the kids."

"I'm done!"

"I'm sorry; I just don't know what or who I want."

I couldn't believe what I had just heard. I was now

dropped to the level of this low-life piece of trash. Her husband, and father of her three children, was nothing to her anymore. Sex was the reason she acted that way when I tried to give her a massage that night for her birthday, and why therapy never got anywhere. As for the rest, I was sick to my stomach, and I couldn't hold back the tears anymore.

I packed up all my belongings as fast as I could while she pleaded for me not to leave her alone. When I finished packing my things I went to the door and I left. I went straight to my best friend's house. I poured my heart out to him and no matter how much I tried to make sense of it and find some sort of release from the pain, I found nothing. I wallowed in it for what seemed like eternity.

That night she showed up in the car with the kids, begging me to come home as she cried and apologized. But I could not bring myself to do it. How could an action like this ever be forgiven? I honestly saw it as impossible.

Over the next few weeks I avoided her as best I could while trying to figure out what the next steps were. I found a divorce lawyer in San Francisco from a friend, so went out multiple times to speak with him, but I couldn't afford his expensive retainer fees. I spoke with countless people who were in my life and most importantly, my brother, my pastor, and God. I honestly had no idea what a man was supposed to do in this situation. Everyone I knew was telling me that I needed to leave her—even my pastor clarifies that if I decided to divorce her, I would have every right biblically to do so. The hardest part in all of this is that I still loved her, and I still cherished my family, and I did not want my children to experience what I had experienced in my life.

It took me a very long time, a lot of reflection, and a lot of clearing some people out of my life to finally come to a decision that I believe now was wrong, but I do not regret in any way. I decided not to leave her. I would find a way to work through the problem. You see, I am a firm believer that everything is fixable, some things are obviously harder than others, but I don't believe anything is impossible. This woman had done things to me that I wouldn't ever wish upon my worst enemy, but I felt that I must exhaust all options of trying to fix it before I left her, or I would regret it at some time in my life. Not only that, but I feel the only thing a man should lose his pride over is his family and his wife.

So with this decision, every guy I knew looked at me like I was an idiot. My close friends started to fall away and looked at me with disgrace for allowing myself to go back like some sick weak dog. What they didn't realize was that it took more strength to do what I was doing than it did to leave at that point. I had to endure criticism from loved ones, co-workers, and clients who knew my story. My outward pride was being chipped away and I was purposely allowing it to happen, because I didn't care what they all thought of me; I never really had in that sense. I knew I wanted my family intact, and I knew there must be a way .i two people are willing to work through the problem; key word being "two".

As we started the process towards fixing our marriage it was apparent that, although she told me she was ready to work on the marriage, she was not mentally prepared or willing to do so. Throughout this early time frame she would cry that she was going through issues at work and she needed him because there was no one else that could work, and that she wanted to play softball after I had made her quit the team because he was on it. She was never all in and it showed.

One Saturday after we had been arguing and were sitting in our living room, I asked her if she still loved me. Her response was one I can still vividly picture in my head. As she lay in a curled up ball on the floor in front of a window with sun shining down on her, while she watched TV, she said, "I don't know." These were three words that I did not want to ever hear. My heart broke and I went numb. I left with my car already packed since I had not unpacked it from the last time we fought and I went to my friend's again; which happened multiple times over the weeks after I found out the truth.

I was on my way to see a client's soccer game in Dublin, a city nearby, where I was able to actually put on a good show and keep it together. I was in a daze the whole day thinking about her response. After the game I was invited over to a buddy's house where a lot of my close friends had gathered to watch the UFC fights. I honestly don't remember the fights, the conversation, or how long I was there. I do remember being so out of it that I barely moved the whole three hours I was there, and it didn't go unnoticed. After the fights were over I immediately got up and headed for the door. On my way out my best friend stopped me and said something that I wish he had never said to me. This entire time, and for the weeks after, I was in a complete daze. It was as if this wasn't really happening to me. It was almost as if I was in a bad dream that I was just hoping to wake up from some day.

He walked with me to the car, looked me in my eyes and said, "Ant, this is your reality." What he meant is that this is REAL. He was telling me that I needed to wake up and understand that this is all really happening, and this is the reality of my life now. I shook my head and got into my car as he went back inside. I started up my car and drove away. I honestly had no idea where I was going, but somehow my body led me to the freeway. As I aimlessly drove, all of a sudden I awoke from my daze and everything hit me like Thor's hammer in the chest. Every ounce of pain

I had felt over the last months of this ordeal came down on my heart collectively at once, like a knife to the heart, and I felt a pain and sorrow more immense and deep than I had ever felt in my life at any point.

I could barely breathe or see the road as tears streamed down my face and I cried uncontrollably. I couldn't shake this feeling that consumed my soul. No one should ever have to feel a pain that strong ever. This was real; and I could not handle it anymore. As I sit here writing this now, my eyes are welling up from digging up these painful memories and feelings. All I could think about was stopping the unbearable pain. How could this be a life I wanted to live anymore? If this is my reality then I don't want it. The only reason I had on this planet for living was my family. Nothing in the world meant more to me than having a solid loving family, which is why I had worked so hard to take care of it. I could not live like this any longer. I wanted to die.

By this time it was around 8 p.m. and I was lost far into the back roads surrounded by nothing but fields, and I made a decision that in my mind was final. I pulled out my phone and sent what I expected to be the last message of my life to my loved ones. "Please tell my children the kind of man I was." As I sent it out my next intentions were to drive and find a store that sold rat poison. The first store I happened upon after I got out of the fields was a gas station, but they didn't carry any. So I parked my car behind the store and sat thinking. By this time I had gotten responses from some people and I honestly cannot recall the conversations I was having, but no part of me intended to change the course I was on. I had made the decision and now it was just a matter of finding a tool.

Then out of nowhere two police cars drove up, shined their lights in my car and instructed me to put my hands up and step out of the vehicle. Apparently my wife had gotten on the phone and called the police and they used GPS to track me down. She had also lost sight of the gun we owned and was scared that I had it, but I did not. After the police frisked me and searched my car filled with my clothes I made up a story that I was leaving her and that's why she had called, because why else would someone looking to take their life pack up the car. They believed the story and let me go on my way, but not before telling me how many people were out looking for me because they cared for me. I got back in my car and found a piece of paper I had received from a pastor we had gone to see during our counseling sessions. It had a scripture on it that made me rethink my plans; that along with the people who the officer said were out looking for me because they cared. The GPS saved my life.

I drove home and when I was pulling up I saw a group of people outside my house on phones, trying to find out where I was. I could see that everyone was happy to see me O.K, but I didn't want to talk to anyone, not even my dad who was there as well. The police made me stay outside while they called the ambulance to take me away to the hospital, without any struggle by me whatsoever, on a 51/50. A 51/50 is what is the code they use to subdue a crazy/uncontrollable person and take them to the hospital. I had hit my rock bottom. After a 30-minute ride while I was willingly strapped to a stretcher inside the ambulance, I arrived at the county hospital. Once check in was complete and I was sitting in a room with people who were apparently either drugged up, or actually crazy, it was clear that I had reached the bottom of my rope. I had come so very close to losing my life. From the heights of my life in professional football, I was now taken all the way down to my knees, ending up in the mental section of the hospital being interview by doctors to make sure I wasn't crazy.

This was a wake-up call. I arrived to the hospital after an uneventful trip in an expensive ambulance. I was placed in a holding room with 5 other people. 3 were wearing tattered clothes that reeked, which made me assume they were homeless, and 2 couldn't stop talking; to themselves. I chose not to speak at all because the nurses already assumed I was crazy and the craziest thing a crazy person can try to explain is that they're not crazy. Soon after I arrived my wife showed up to take me home, probably the last person I wanted to see at that moment, but I had no other choice than to go. The only positive thing was that there was nowhere to go but up from there.

The time immediately after that night is a loss to me, and it's probably for the best. We had a very in-depth conversation about our past and our future. Sold me that she was sorry and wanted to really try to fix the marriage this time, but she didn't want to go to therapy anymore. So we found a program that we could do at home and we gave it a try. In fact it actually started working. I was still hanging in there and having a horrible time at work and in life, but this started to help and make things better.

In late 2011, we took a trip to Disneyland with her family and I must say it was the best three days we had together in the three years leading up to that day. It was an amazing trip, and when we got back things were actually moving in the right direction, although far from perfect. Then at the end of the year when things were finally looking up life came around to show its ugly side again.

I received a call one night that my mom had been taken to the hospital because she wasn't doing well and hadn't slept in days. She had gotten to the point where she was so tired from lack of sleep that she was essentially dreaming awake, and no one had any idea what was going on. When I heard about it I hurried to the hospital with my wife. When we arrived it was the scariest sight I had seen. My mom didn't even recognize anyone and she wasn't improving at all. I thought she was going to die. Sitting there watching my family members cry was excruciating to watch.

After an hour or so my wife left and I stayed behind to be with my family. While we were there praying that my mom would be O.K, I wondered why one of my sisters hadn't shown up. After checking Facebook, I noticed that she was inviting people over to her house to drink that night. When I read it I decided I should reach out and let her know that with mom being the hospital it was inappropriate. The response wasn't what I expected, in fact it was one of the most hurtful things I had ever heard from her. She said I should mind my own business and that she wished I had gone through with killing myself because I deserved to have my wife cheat on me. She went on to say that I only wished Grace was my real mom, like mom was to her. I couldn't believe what she had said.

After a short back and forth, I dropped it. It wasn't worth it. To this day I have never brought up the conversation; it's just not worth the argument that would ensue. To make things worse that wasn't the worst part of what happened in my life over the next few days.

After leaving the hospital I was feeling sad, hurt, and I just needed my wife to be with me that night. I got in my car and tried to call my wife who had only left a little while earlier, but I could not reach her. I called and called and called and I couldn't find her, I eventually got a text from her that she was going to hang out with one of her girlfriends; she said she didn't want to be with me that night and just needed some space. I told her I needed her but she never responded. I drove home and had found no one to talk to in my time of need. I went into my garage, got into my car, and fell asleep, sad and alone, praying that my mom would survive her ordeal.

The next morning I awoke in my car in my garage and went to see my mom again. I found out that she was actually doing better. I was so happy to hear that. I also heard back from my wife who asked me to come home to see her; she was for some reason in a more positive mood. I asked what she did and she said, "nothing big," and didn't go into it any further. I happened to go into the kitchen and on the counter was a half-empty bottle of vodka. I immediately asked who drank all of it and she said she had. She said she had taken the kids out to her mom's in the city and got a hotel in concord so that she could just sit and drink alone. She showed me the receipts and the bank statement for the hotel room she had gotten. Although it seemed odd, I didn't dig into it further because she said she needed the time to clear her mind and now felt good moving on. She said that after she saw how my mom was with my dad, she didn't want to ever be in that situation without me. The words made me feel great for the first time in years. Sadly, though, that feeling would be fleeting in less than 48 hours.

Two nights later we happened to be shopping at a target in the neighboring city and were just randomly walking around the store. I noticed a funny look on her face, as she seemed to be scoping out the store. I was not thinking anything of it and then I saw something that made my blood turn cold. Cyn's roommates, who had watched my kids, according to my wife, while she would go into his bedroom, were in the store. These were people she actually worked with, and were her friends as well. I later found out that on the way in she had seen his car and she thought it was him, but they all shared a car since they each couldn't afford to buy one. I struggled to hold back my anger as she started to grab me and walk me to the front so we could buy our things and get out of the store. I didn't say anything and they didn't know I had seen them. To my wife's dismay they walked up to the front to check out as well, and they finally noticed me. I couldn't help but stare directly at them just waiting for them to look at me and say something. Cyn's roommate looked at me and I could tell he didn't know what to do or say so I yelled out, "What?" at the top of my lungs in the store. My wife immediately grabbed me by the arm and started to drag me out of the store, even though I was fighting to stay,

wanting him to say just one word to me, which would have
sent me off in a flurry.

What kind of people would a person consider friends
who would condone an affair, so much so that they would
watch the children while you did your dirt? They disgusted me and still disgust me as humans. We got in the car
and the first thing I told her was to never do something
like that again. If I want to say something to those scums,
I will do it. In hindsight I am glad she did what she did
because I was acting emotionally and nothing good would
have come of it.

We got home and I couldn't shake the feeling of anger.
Yet again I was subjected to seeing people who looked at
me as less than a man. All of my life I had fought so hard
to be an upstanding person so that no one could hold anything over me, so that I had my pride respectfully intact.
She had done so much out in the open that I couldn't walk
around with my head held high anymore, because I was
the guy to laugh at since my wife had slept around on me.
She gave my pride away to the world like it was worth
nothing. I could barely sleep that night and then something weird happened. At 3 in the morning I got a weird
feeling in my stomach that I couldn't shake; it was the feeling that I needed to check her phone. I slowly and quietly
got up from my side of the bed and walked around to the
other side to grab her phone, making sure not to wake her

up. I opened the phone and looked at the recent apps, one happened to be Facebook, so I opened it. Once I opened it, I could see that she had been messaging someone, so I looked to see who. It was the guy we had seen at the store just hours earlier. My heart began beating faster and faster as I opened the messages to see what had been written.

"Hey, "I'm sorry about that earlier, when Anthony yelled in the store. I know you guys have nothing to do with anything that happened between me and him, and Anthony doesn't know what went down. Only me and him know what really went down between the two of us."

"It's cool, I ain't trippin" he responded. "Me and Cyn talked it out though. We spent the night together the other night and just figured we'll keep it simple for now, sorry again"

The second I read the last line my heart sunk again and anger started to well up in me darker than it had before. Not only had she lied to me about hanging out with her friend that night, but she in fact had spent the evening with him! MONTHS after she supposedly hadn't talk to him, they spent the night together?! I tore the covers off of her and called her every single name I could think of. She didn't know what was going on so I read the messages back to her as loud as possible so it was crystal clear what was going on. She tried to explain everything away and say that she didn't stay with him, but that because the break up with him had been so abrupt, she never had a chance to clean it up and move forward. After seeing my mom she said she needed a clean break, so she got a hotel in a distant city, drove in to see him and talk to him in his car, then drove back to her hotel to finish off a half of a bottle, and not be too drunk to drive home in the morning.

I didn't buy it then and I don't to this day. I have zero proof, but my heart tells me they shared that bottle in her hotel room two cities away where no one would recognize them. At this point I was past crying. She kept demanding that I give her the phone back and I told her the only way she was getting it back was if she left my home right then and there. She refused and I kept insisting. After 15 minutes of going back and forth, I got her to step outside and I gave her the phone as I locked her out of the house in the cold. She didn't deserve to be in that home with my children and me. She called the police and they eventually came and said that because she was on the lease she was entitled to stay, and the crazy part was that the entire time she acted like she didn't have a care in the world; like she was better than the whole situation, like she was better than me. Regardless of how good she felt she was, I locked my door and her butt slept on the couch that night.

The next day I tried to move past it again but I couldn't. Notice that I have yet to say I fully forgave her at this time because I hadn't, although I was trying, I couldn't. How can you when new things pop up so frequently, one after the other. I was done; I gathered the money I needed to go see my lawyer to get a divorce. I was halfway out the door when she did something she hadn't done the entire time we had been arguing. She broke. For the first time she opened up in ways she never had. She apologized for all the pain she had caused, how she had hurt me so ruthlessly, and that she didn't know what it was, but she couldn't stop because it felt like a drug she couldn't shake. She asked me to give it one more chance, then asked if we could just take a trip with the family out to Oregon where we had gone to college. She said she just wanted to get away from the area and go back to the last place she remembers us being truly happy. After a lot of reluctance I agreed.

The next week, after the holidays, we took a trip north to Oregon. The trip STILL almost didn't happen. By this time my family wanted nothing to do with her for obvious reasons, so when I went to my aunt's house with my kids for Christmas eve she went to her best friend's house. I got home around 11p.m. and put my kids to bed alone, since she wasn't anywhere to be found and she wasn't answering her phone. So I started wrapping presents once the kids were down and about 10 minutes into it, she comes stumbling through the door. I looked up to see her and she told me that she had to go upstairs to rest because she had eaten a weed cookie and was too high to help. She had come home high on Christmas Eve from her best friend's house. I was PISSED! I would have yelled at her but I wasn't going to let her ruin the kid's night by me yelling and waking them up.

I texted her friend, who she said she was with, and got angry at her for letting my wife do that on this night of all nights. Her friend literally didn't care and in fact got mad at me for reaching out to her. What kind of best friend LETS you do that and doesn't stop you??!

Tanya eventually came downstairs and I couldn't even look at her while we finished wrapping the gifts for the kids, and then went to sleep. I couldn't imagine how she could even do that. It was Christmas and for the sake of the kids, I let it go. I acted like it never happened.

The holidays passed awkwardly and we were set to take our trip to Oregon. At this time my friends and colleagues still couldn't fathom why I was even giving this woman any of my time. They looked at me with a sense of disgrace. No matter what I said, no one understood, and honestly, neither did I. We packed up our car and kids and we set off for a trip to Eugene Oregon to try to recapture all the memories that, at one time, had built up such a strong bond between us over the years. For the two of us Eugene combines so many memories it's hard to even recount them all. To be honest the trip was a blast. We got a rinky-dink little hotel room in the heart of town and went on a tour of all the places where we had spent so much time. With the kids we visited all of the old places where we had lived, went to watch movies in the old theaters, visited familiar restaurants, shopped at the Goodwill, got tours of the sports facilities, and so much more.

The trip was doing its intended job of getting us away from the town, people, and environment that was a cancer to us, and was blatantly hindering our ability to reconnect. This way there were no familiar faces, no judgments, no bad acquaintances, and it seemed like all was right in the world for once in so very long. The short week came to a close and we left Oregon feeling closer than we had been in many years. We got home and started getting back to our normal lives, but sadly, the closeness wouldn't last.

Just as had happened in life prior when the rigors of a normal schedule of life came down upon us, and the people in our lives re-entered the picture, little by little things went back to the way they had been. We eventually started to argue all the time so decide to, yet again, try going to see a therapist. She said she thought I was not letting her live it down when I actually was trying to. It was all still fresh so it was nearly impossible to act as though it had never happened. She eventually hated going to therapy because she felt like it was just a focus on her mistakes and she got to the point where she'd completely check out. The pressure of trying to fix the marriage shut her off completely and all she wanted to do was escape it all. She was visibly tired of putting in the effort necessary to fix the mistakes she had made, and she would make statements saying it would be easier to just chock it all up and start new with someone else instead of fixing what she had broken. She had never been a person of strength, that was always my role, but no one can be strong for another person, it's something that people must harbor for themselves, especially in a marriage.

One night at 1a.m. she decided to get up and get dressed and leave in the middle of the night, literally the middle of the night. I asked where she was going and she just said to a girlfriend's house. She left and didn't answer her phone at all the entire night, even though I kept calling her repeatedly. She eventually walked in the door the next morning at 10a.m. as if nothing happened.

One fateful day she decided she didn't want to go to therapy that afternoon. She told me it was because she was getting her hair done and she had forgotten about the appointment. When I told her to forget about it because it was either that or therapy, she chose her hair. I was devastated AGAIN.

Three years I had been drug through this hell of rollercoaster of ups and downs, and after I finally feel we had made some progress, I come to realize it was false. What I didn't find until later that evening was that she was in fact going out with her friends that night and hadn't told me.

We argued about how I felt that she was not doing things becoming of a woman in her position, and she again didn't care, as she got dressed, left me with the kids, and selfishly went out on the town again. She didn't answer the phone when I called and the sickening feeling of feeling unimportant crept back into my heart and mind. I couldn't handle it anymore.

The next morning I woke up and check my Instagram account only to see pictures of Tanya in a bar hugged up next to guys I didn't know. So I got pissed again, for obvious reasons, but I had no one to blame but myself for staying so long at that point. I finally packed up all my belongings and decided it was time to move on. I called a friend of mine whose girlfriend had a small, 400 square foot studio in the back of her house, which didn't even have a kitchen. I moved in.

The path to progress had finally been started. One day I drove Tanya out to a place in a nearby city where a woman would help us file our divorce papers and start the process of me doing something I had never believed in. We drove to a woman's house who dealt with helping couples file without having to pay the high legal fees. Tanya cried and said it wasn't what she wanted, but her words and her actions were in a battle daily, and I was tired of being the fool who had to experience the outcome of her daily battle between what her mind and heart wanted. The pain had gotten to a point where I was unable to handle it anymore. It was time to start the process of letting go and moving on with my life.

We walked into this woman's home and discussed the process and how it would transpire. This woman went on to degrade me for some odd reason for not making a bunch of money. I had to actually hold back from cursing her out for her candid discussion of her skewed view of me. We discussed custody of the children, separation of materials belongings, and just about anything you can imagine a couple would have to divide. We walked into that house a couple and left as two divided individuals with the start of the divorce process completed. I filed for divorce and moved forward with my life the best I could

I wish I could say that the process was simple and smooth and that I never looked back, but I would be lying. From day one I struggled with it. I had gone from having my kids every night in my home and being able to say goodnight and kiss them on their heads, to being alone and sleeping alone in an empty studio like a college student every other day and every other weekend when I didn't have my kids half of the time. My heart hurt because I had lost everything that meant anything to me. At the same time that all this was going on in my personal life, I was, in fact, somehow able to keep the gym alive and it was starting to thrive. At no point over the first 4 years of the gyms existence had there been a sense of solidarity in my life. The gym had never honestly had a fully focused man at its helms from the start, but for some reason my love for my profession, my genuine caring for my clients, my careful planning, and my insatiable work ethic, based on a confidence in my ability to succeed, allowed me to build a gym even against the odds.

I had a wife who brought me to my knees in life, I had business failures that almost ended the dream early on, I had horrible employees, and I had setback after setback in a downtrodden economy. But I was able to not only keep it alive, I was able to now move it into a large 8,250 square foot facility that was in fact the largest training facility our area had ever seen. The place was big, beautiful, and the feeling of accomplishment was amazing. I had a staff of nineteen, hundreds of happy clients, and the place was booming. I remember one night in early winter sitting at the front desk with my manager looking at the dozens of people packed into the place having a great time. It was a culmination of years of hard work and effort, physically and emotionally, as my life on the outside was a consistent drain. I would leave the big beautiful gym and drive home, down the street, to a studio not fit for a college student. I was a grown man and I had my three children sleeping next to my bed all bundled up on a queen size air mattress because that's the only room I had to spare. Not to mention that I couldn't afford a bigger place on such short notice of having to move.

Life was so uncomfortable that I felt like I was hanging on by a thread almost every day. I was finally out on my own with a thriving business, but every part of me felt like a loser in life. I was going nowhere and all the things I valued were intact, but so unorganized that I went to sleep with a weird feeling in the pit of my stomach every single night. I was uncomfortable with life and I was unable to rectify it.

If everything wasn't already bad enough, things progressively got worse before they got better. I started to drink beer every night at home just to relax and clear my mind after long days, and I found out my ex had gotten a new boyfriend. The way I found out is that one night after dropping the kids off at her at her house around 9:30, I went out and around midnight saw her drunk in a bar. I was furious and told her to get home to the kids. I had come to find out that she drove, and although I am not sure I believe it, she had arranged to be picked up by her new boyfriend after I scolded her, even though I had no power to. Now the fact that she was with someone else wasn't actually all that new to me, so I wasn't bothered by it as much as one would think. What bothered me was the fact that I now had to deal with another man in this world being present in my children's life against my desire, and I had done nothing to deserve it.

I had zero control over what happened when I wasn't present, but as a father, knowing another man is tucking your kids into bed, it's a horrible feeling, especially when you know you're a good loving father. I hated it inside, but I had to dig inside to deal with the whole situation as an adult the best I could. It's something I have to think about and deal with every day knowing that my kids will have another father someday. To keep away from having to focus on issues like this I did what most newly single people do in their lives at the age of 28, I focused hugely on work and going out. Both of which are not healthy in large doses.

I spent more than fourteen hours a day at work just so that I wasn't alone with my thoughts. I went out on the weekends with friends and had a few drinks just to enter back into the scene to see what it was like. I had literally never been to a bar single in my life and it was an experience I didn't in fact enjoy. I had given up the desire to drink and party at a young age and even now the feeling didn't return. I was floating around in life and it was driving me crazy. I was on such unstable ground and didn't like the unsettling feeling of it all. I had no one to come home to, no support base, a rickety home to live in, and although I was known in the community, I was essentially living in a shack and I internally didn't feel fit to be a leader. I have never admitted this until now, but I cannot fathom how in the world the gym managed to stay alive and not fail during these times. I can only attest that it was due to good planning and execution on mine, and my team's, side. The only thing I did have intact was my desire to make sure my staff was happy and that my clients were served. I can only assume that my management skills and God's grace saw me through those trying times.

After a few nights of taking part in some things that I truly wish I could take back, I had gotten to the end of my road of desiring to be winging it through life. Business was getting harder to run as I was wearing thin inside, and dealing with my ex and her craziness was taking a toll on my heart daily. I missed my three amazing children any time they weren't with me and I just needed a base to stand on once again. Not to mention that my run-ins with women were getting tiring and I started feeling horrible as a person from the sexual experiences I was having; it was not in my nature to have multiple sexual partners.

Then all of a sudden something came into my life that would give me that base. My aunt Anne set me up to meet a new girl named Sarah that she thought would be a perfect fit for me. I remember the very first conversation we had on January 4th that lasted for hours and hours. I felt like I could talk to this girl and never get tired of it. Sarah was amazing to me and the feeling was mutual. I felt all the feelings I had felt before, and they were possibly even stronger than I had felt before. She was one of the most beautiful women I had ever met and she had a very caring and warm heart. After talking with her for about a month I knew that I wanted her in my life. We took a trip to Seattle and for the first time we told each other we were in love. To be completely honest, I did love her. Sarah also felt the same for me and because of it we pushed the pace faster than I think we should have in hindsight.

Sarah lived two hours from me so when I got off work at 8:30 p.m., I'd go home and take a shower, drive two hours to see her, hang out, then drive back home just in time to go to work at 5:30 a.m. the next day. I got to the point where I was tired of traveling so much so I brought up the idea of having her move in with me. She agreed and I was on cloud nine. We moved in together into a three-bedroom house in my town and we were starting our journey of life together. We had a ton of amazing memories together and I had a blast. We went to Seattle, Puerto Rico, Washington D.C. and on hikes together. This journey, however, wouldn't end the way I hoped.

What I didn't take into account was all the dynamics of life that had not been figured out between us during the three shorts months leading up to our moving in to-gether. She had come from a different style of living, she liked things a certain way, and my kids were a complete new adventure for this young 25-year-old girl. She had said early on that it was not a problem for her at all, but the kids turned out to be a huge issue. In fact, it was the combination of the kids and my ex-wife that eventually ruined the situation. She couldn't wrap her mind around the fact that I was always going to have my kids with me and that my ex would always be present in their lives. I tried with everything I had to get her to understand that my primary relationship would come first, so that I could model for my children what a happy relationship should look like, and where the children stood in relation to that. I love my children to death, but I feel it is O.K to put my girlfriend above them in certain instances so that they will understand how to do the same when they get married someday—to see what it means to love and cherish their spouse. I wanted her to feel fully accepted by me, so I did so with my actions, but she wasn't able to see it, sadly.

What really strained the relationship on top of the kids was my ex-wife and her crazy actions. Due to the fact that I had a new girlfriend, I stopped all communication with her outside of the needed communication about the kids, and she hated it. When I wouldn't joke around with her anymore and didn't have the casual conversations, she would to get pissed off. In fact she absolutely hated the fact that I wasn't talking to her, and that I had a new girlfriend. Sadly, it got to the point where she filed for more custody of our children, dragging me through a battle that was hurtful for my kids, my new relationship, and me. It turns out my ex-wife still had feelings for me even though she was in a relationship. She was using the kids against me. It was her way of trying to strain my new relationship because she didn't want to see me in it.

Sadly her plan worked, and my new girlfriend got to the point where everything was too stressful for her to deal with. I could see it taking a toll and for our sake I broke it off and she moved back home. To this day I always wonder what would have turned out if we had taken it slow and if she didn't allow my ex to get to her. There's no way to know how things would have turned out, but I did learn invaluable lessons about myself, life, and how to handle situations like that in the future. My ex-wife accomplished her goal, but honestly, I wasn't angry at her because I understood how it must have felt for her since I had been in those shoes. It didn't help that on my 29th birthday, ten years after meeting my father, he told me that he did, in fact, know that I had existed my entire life. Life never failed to kick me when I was down. Things eventually subsided and life got back to a normal pace.

* * *

The solidarity I discovered by being with this new girl allowed me to start getting back to my old self. I was gaining confidence in my abilities again, and started to blossom professionally. I had come out of my slump and regained my pride from the loss that I had experienced. I no longer wanted to sit and stew about my past, I wanted to regain myself and move forward. I had by this time been able to run a successful gym for years, become a best-selling author in a book aimed at youth athletes where I talk about my life, spoken around the country, trained thousands of clients and multiple professional athletes, and I had begun consulting for a billion dollar a year company. I was getting back to being myself. In fact after everything had smoothed out with my ex, she approached me a year later about trying to work things out and get back together. An offer I considered, but she would in fact not be prepared to work the way it would be necessary for me to truly consider it a possibility.

I was feeling great but then I discovered that I was internally starting to feel as though something was out place. I couldn't figure it out because at work I was able to sustain a full corporation and it was financially doing well; I had a lot of happy clients, my kids were happy and healthy, my ex wanted me back, I was very content being alone,, and all was right again. For some reason though I felt as though something was lacking in my life and that I wanted more. I started thinking back to what I had promised myself years earlier about wanting to be great. I had been working in a community that didn't appreciate my abilities and experience and only cared about the price of the service, not the value. I was only able to reach so many people, and my heart wanted to reach and help so many more people than I was finding myself able to. I questioned myself, wanting to know if what I was doing in life was truly GREAT. Was I using all the skills God blessed me with in this life to achieve the greatest things I could? The answer was no, and then something happened that gave me the answer and solution I was looking for in my life. I happened upon what I truly believe to be my purpose.

Years earlier I had gotten to the point where I wanted to take my own life, but I wouldn't realize the profound effect it would have on my life so many years later. About two years later while at a party surrounded by all of my friends, I was simply talking about life and all the things I had endured and experienced. I spent hours reflecting upon my life. I was a child brought up through a situation that would break the spirit of some of the strongest people I know, but I came out positive minded. I found out what work ethic in life meant at a young age and it allowed me to comprehend what it takes to work for what you truly want in life. I had a child in one the worst situations you could have a child in, by being out of state, in college, and unmarried. I had been through deaths and losses of close family members. I fought through many hardships in my first career in the NFL, I opened a business that is truly a struggle every day, and I endured an affair so bad that even my close friends and family are amazed that one of the three involved didn't lose their life in the process.

In all honesty, I harbor no anger or hatred towards anyone involved in causing me any pain. I genuinely have a positive care for even my ex-wife, who I believe was in a bad place in her life and I failed her by not being able to help her save her from herself when it was needed. Regardless of what blame I try to place on her, the truth is I may carry just as much blame for not seeing the signs and making the changes necessary to rectify the situation earlier. She tells me now that everything she blamed on me was all a lie to justify her actions and that she acted selfishly for years. I In fact, couldn't have done anything to stop it, but I don't truly believe that. It takes a lot of pride swallowing to admit that, but it's the truth. No one experiences what I experienced without having some part of responsibility, even if it's miniscule. She is a loving mother to my kids and although some would believe she does not deserve forgiveness, she is truly forgiven in my eyes and we are now able to joke and comically discuss the situation and all that transpired.

The reason I bring this up is because at the end of this night, one of my close friends said something to me that has truly changed my perception of the purpose of my life forever. The statement made was simple yet very profound and powerful to me. My friend said to me in confidence that when he heard about what was going on with me trying to end my life, he literally got sick to his stomach. He said, "Anthony you're my hero." I was floored and taken back by his words. I honestly didn't know how to respond to the statement. I didn't know how to accept it in all honesty.

"How am I you're hero?" I asked.

"Because of all you have gone through in life and all you have been able to achieve in life with the amazingly positive attitude you have." He may not know it himself, but I actually have a GREAT deal of respect for him as a man, so this coming from him was unexpected but greatly appreciated. I was astonished at his perception of me because I honestly had never heard anyone say something like that to me before. It took me by surprise. His words actually made me think about life and what it was all about. More so, what my life was all about.

You see, I was already in a business directed towards helping people improve their lives. I have spent the last ten years of my life trying to help people in the area that I have the most technical knowledge to help them, the fitness and training world. I have helped literally thousands of people improve their lives through the physical attributes, but all the while I wasn't cognitive of the area that I was truly helping them improve in; their minds and hearts. I came to find that although I got a certain sense of pride by helping someone improve their speed and agility in sports, or lose the fat they had been trying to lose for a while; I honestly got the most enjoyment by seeing their overall life improve. If I am lucky I may get to help someone hands on for twelve hours a month at most, usually. The massive changes in my client's lives, however, come in all the other house spent living throughout that month. What I mean is that I want to see their lives fully change for the better, which requires more than just increasing strength and losing weight.

My friend had opened up a perspective of me, beyond what I truly had seen for myself prior to his statement. I am living my life in a way that many people are unable to understand. A life that is contrary to what someone would expect of a person who endured my hardships. A life that is full of joy and happiness due to my perspective on all the things that have happened in my life, and all the life tools I have learned through experience and gaining wisdom. I am living a life that is a beacon of hope for others who happen upon it, a life that I now feel obligated, and proud to share with the world. If I could unknowingly be his hero and help him want to do better in life, I wonder how many people I could help if I reached out to the world and shared my life with them.

In 2012 I took a trip to Monterey for a business retreat with my colleagues from the fitness industry and in one of our many meetings something special happened. I was listening to a colleague of mine describe how she wanted to open a fitness business. She listed off all the things she had already accomplished, which included having clients, having funding, having a location, a business plan, and all of our support, but she couldn't pull the trigger because she just wanted to be sure it was going to be successful. In my mind I couldn't figure what was standing in her way. In the most respectful way I said, "You have all the tools in place that you need, but you don't have the most important thing. You don't believe in yourself enough to do it. There isn't going to be any guarantee that it will work. I had literally nothing in place when I wanted to open my gym and I still went forward with it."

"How could you do that?" she asked.

"I guess I just trusted my hustle." I said. "I knew that at some point it would fail and I trusted in my ability to make it work when it did fail."

One of my other colleagues said, "That's good, you should use that Anthony." I must say that I liked it. Throughout my life I had learned very clearly that life is what happens between your plans, so you have to have a deep sense of trust in your work ethic to overcome any unforeseen obstacles that will definitely pop up. I had to learn how to build a thriving business from scratch without any guidance, but it never scared me because I knew that I would work my butt off to make it succeed, no matter what was thrown my way. TRUST YOUR HUSTLE WAS BORN.

At first I didn't really know what I would do with the phrase and it kind of sat on the back burner of my mind just stewing around. Then came the day when my friend made his statement and everything kind of came together in my mind somehow. I have always had this burning desire to help people in my life, which is why I opened up my gym, but I started to think deeper after I had that conversation. I liken myself to a pincushion; God's pincushion I say. As I think back to all the things that have been placed in my life as obstacles, I start I wonder why I was put through all of them year after year with almost no reprieve. Then I realized that I have a unique ability to see the world differently than most people. Not only that, but I have the self-confidence to share my stories without fear of judgment or a loss in self-worth.

People need to know that a person like me exists, because I have found people like myself who showed me the light when it was needed most. A pincushion is able to hold hundreds of tiny little pins and needles that, if used a certain way, can be taken out and cause people pain by poking by them. In this case, as a pincushion, I could take all of my needles, being life troubles, and use them against the world by causing other people pain. I could very easily be a horrible father to my children, demean others, hold grudges, and try to make the world pay for what it did to me. Or I could do what I have chosen to do in my life. I have chosen to take the needles—all the pain caused to me over the years—and take them out, thread the needles with a golden thread, and use those very same pain points to help mend the tapestries of the lives of others.

I want to take the pain caused to me and use it to make other peoples' lives as great as possible, because I truly see the beauty the world has to offer, even if the world tries to hide it. The world does not need any more anger and bitterness, what the world needs is joy, happiness, and appreciation for what we have. Anything and everything a person wants out of this amazing blessing we call life can be attained when they figure out that all they have to do is learn to believe in themselves, by understanding how to trust their hustle. So many people are unhappy because they want, but that increases exponentially because they realize the fact that they are capable of getting it. But they don't believe they are capable of putting forth the work it would take to achieve it. It's a vicious cycle because they are already unhappy because they want something, but they are doubly unhappy because they despise themselves for not being able to work hard enough to go after it. So we slump down in our lives and slide by because we don't trust that we have what it takes to achieve great things in life.

I am a personal walking talking testament to the fact that everything a person wants out of life is attainable if they learn how to go after it. No one should simply "exist" in life, because everyone deserves the right to be great in whatever way he or she deems fit. My goal in life is to help people accomplish that goal. Everyone wants something different in life, and it is never my intention to tell someone what is and is not worthy of being great. For some people its building a great business, so I help them do that, for other people its learning how to be a better father or mother, to others it's how to be great athletes, great coaches, or to simply find out what they want to do with their lives and how to go after what they believe will truly bring them happiness.

I have helped thousands of people over the years not only achieve better physical attributes, but better mentalities because we helped figure out what they wanted to do with their lives beyond the sets and reps of exercise. I truly believe I was placed on this earth to simply help people find a way to live the best possible life they can by eliminating excuses and learning how to take the necessary actionable steps to move closer to their dream lives every day.

I love the saying, "A life in service to others is the rent we should pay to live on this earth," because it ties to my heart so deeply. I now want to live a life in service to others by helping them get out of their own way, to go after the life they want to live. I can tell you with a full belief from the depths of my soul that all things are attainable in your life when you learn to TRUST YOUR HUSTLE.

CHAPTER 8:

TRUST YO**U**R HUSTLE

In all troublesome situations there are three types of people who come out on the back end. 1) The person who dies physically or emotionally from a traumatic event and never recovers. 2) The person who gets through the situation but stays emotionally stuck in it because they become so comfortable and used to the pain that they find a sense of normalcy in it, and don't want or know how to move past it. 3) The person who survives the event and grows STRONGER and WISER from it. I am number three and I will never fall into number 1 or 2 at any point in my life ever again. What I have found is that my ability to do this comes from a different perspective I now have in life. Earlier I stated that "Perspective Precedes

Enlightenment," and I fully believe that. Unless you see your problems in a different light, or different perspective, you will never get to the "Ah ha" moments where you see the problem differently.

My perspective from my many years of trials has become vastly different than the average persons. I LOVE my life and what I have been able to accomplish, but that ability is very possible to be had by YOU. I learned early in life that no matter what came my way I had to trust in myself. I had to TRUST MY HUSTLE. My life has been a string of obstacles almost one after another, but through all of them I was able to trust in my ability to work through any problem. I have an undying faith in my personal will power to succeed against any odds stacked against me, because I have been able to prove to MYSELF that I am able to succeed when I trust in my abilities and see things through to the very end; the key word being "trust."

TRUST is a unique thing. There can be outward trust in terms of trusting another being outside of myself. This could be a spouse, friend, sibling, and even your version of your God. Then the inward trusting of one's self, the most important one in my mind. Not being able to trust yourself is a difficult truth for some people, much like an alcoholic doesn't trust himself or herself around alcohol, or a smoker can't resist cigarettes. Regardless, the question is, Can that person be "TRUSTED"? For that to be possible you have **T**o **R**eally **U**nderstand **S**omeone's **T**endencies **E**ntering **D**ecisions. To be "TRUSTED" you have to deep down almost KNOW what that person will do when faced with a decision, because TRUST is only tested when a decision is to be made. Will that person do what you have "TRUSTED" them to do, or will they fall short and break your trust? Will your friend or spouse uphold your trust when tested? Can you TRUST yourself in the situation you've placed yourself in? The truth is, there is no way to be completely sure. In my many life experiences I have found that it HURTS very badly when others break your trust. What I am personally sure of is that when I break my own trust, it hurts me much more than when others do, because in that situation there is no one to blame but myself. Self-blame occurs in so many people's hearts every day and it stops them from picking up and moving forward in life for years, and sometimes forever.

The silver lining is this; ALL things can be mended with time and actions. So I have found that freedom lies in learning to forgive and move forward to let that person BUILD back up your trust, whether it's someone who broke your trust, or the person staring back at you in the mirror.

The true concept of Trust Your Hustle lies in that very principle. So many people tell others to "just believe in yourself" because "you have it in you to do great things." These are statements I FULLY believe, but how many times have you heard that? How many times have you said or posted quotes that you fail to live by? I could tell you until I am blue in the face that you can achieve great things, but the outcome would be the same every time, because it would be rooted in the same conscious belief, or lack thereof, in yourself. You would get all pumped up for now, and maybe it will last a couple days if you're lucky, but then it will fade away. Even the most confident people have those dark moments when they're alone with their thoughts where they doubt themselves. Why? What I know is that millions of people hear powerful messages on a daily basis but are stuck for some reason and cannot find out what they need to move forward in their lives with everlasting motivation and drive. They wonder why they are unable to make the breakthrough. They know their ability to succeed exists because of the many examples of people going from rags to riches, and they KNOW they have the resources and abilities to achieve their goals, but they STILL fall short. I believe it is their inability to trust in their own abilities to achieve the things they want in life that ultimately leads to their demise.

Belief is rooted in trust, and without it no belief can exist. It's because their track record of failures in life has told them they are incapable of trusting themselves to actually complete the tasks at hand needed to reach the end, so they lack a self-belief in the ability to succeed. They look at the path ahead and so fully want to walk it, but they are stuck at the first step because they feel like they are looking at a path they have walked before, one they were unable to finish, whether they know this or not. Their fear and lack of self-belief comes from a lack of trust in themselves. Fear will always hinder their ability to move forward because they don't TRUST themselves, and in turn don't trust their hustle or work ethic to see it through to the end. Until they can build a trust in themselves, they will never fully believe that they can do what others have SHOWN them they are capable of doing.

Trust leads to belief, belief leads to faith, and faith quintessentially is HOPE, and hope is a dangerously positive thing because it has no bounds. When you can learn to trust your ability to overcome obstacles, you then start to have a belief in your abilities to accomplish greater things. Once you have a deep-seeded belief, you can grow a tree of faith. Now for me, I see faith both as spiritual and non-spiritual, but it can be surmised to represent both. Faith is a "belief" that something good will come of my devotion to working towards a cause, even though I cannot visibly see the outcome. In spiritual faith you believe a God you cannot see with your own eyes, or touch with your own hands, but you believe him to be real. Some people believe so whole-heartedly that they give their lives, and take others' lives, for their religion. Faith in the sense of working towards a goal does not differ. When I have faith in my ability to succeed, I am going to work whole heartedly toward an end result that I cannot see or touch yet, but I know is coming as long as I continue to work long enough and hard enough. This ability creates a feeling that has allowed men and women to survive situations that would in fact have killed them. This feeling is the all-powerful HOPE. Hope, when planted with a strong foundation of belief and faith, will endure for eternity if necessary. Hope is the ultimate knowing that something is possible.

Every situation in life has a hopeful possibility, even when something seems impossible. Whenever something seems perfect and/or impossible, it cannot be in the very sense of the word. The pure fact that nothing and no one is "perfect" is a testament to this. So no matter how small the possibility, it still exists. Therein lies the possibility that nothing is impossible.

A person must learn to build trust in themselves and their abilities, or they will forever be fighting an uphill battle. The way people usually get into these spiraling messes is because they look at life's problems like a cat with a sock on its head. Now I know that sounds odd, but bear with me. When I was a kid I remember one time when I placed a sock over my cats head to see what would happen. To my amazement the cat did something that sticks in my head to this day. The cat started to quickly back up as fast as possible to try its hardest to get itself out of the predicament it was in. This cat backed up so fiercely and without stopping that it literally backed itself up a wall trying to reverse itself out of the sock. What if that cat backed itself out of a window or off a cliff? Imagine now how you feel when you have a problem that you are dealing with, or a situation that makes you feel deathly afraid and uncomfortable. What do you do? Do you back up like the cat? If you are like most people, your reaction is to back up as fast as possible and just get out of the problem to stop the crappy feeing you are having. But when you are finally removed and you look back at the problem, a sense of regret sinks in because you notice that either 1) You wish you had the strength to endure the problem and show the strength you have to overcome it, 2) You missed an opportunity to BUILD strength from going through a hardship in life, or 3) You backed yourself into an even worse problem than the one you started in. If the cat were smart it would avoid the possibility of those setbacks by simply stopping from backing up, place its paws on the sock, and pull its head out of the sock, then stand up right in the same spot it started in, triumphant in its success.

Imagine how much trust that cat would have from overcoming a problem like that so in the future it knew it could succeed. Imagine how much trust, belief, and faith you would have in yourself in the future if you knew you had overcome a huge problem in your past. Would you have the feeling that you actually COULD believe in yourself like so many people tell you that you should?

In my life trusting my hustle has been a reality. There have been so many struggles placed in my path that I have overcome. I now have a deep-rooted faith in my ability to succeed in any situation. I have "hope" that supersedes any difficulties that arise. My hope is rooted in my faith in not only my God, but also in the abilities my God has given me to endure my life's hardships. To date I have not failed at anything I have truly given my all to, but the key to that statement lies in the word "ALL." I can't guarantee that if I gave my all I will have succeeded, but I can guarantee that if I didn't give my all I will most definitely have failed.

This is the distinct reason why I loathe laziness in life. It literally hurts my heart when I see or hear about people who are too lazy to go after their dream in life, and then to make things worse they'll either make excuses as to why they cannot go after it, they'll complain about not being happy where they are in life, or both. How can you gripe and moan daily about the position you are in in life, but have no conscious thought to use the many tools at your disposal to make your situation change for the better? I will never fully comprehend that mindset, but it is my mission to try to understand it better so that I can find a way to help those people stuck in that mindset.

So in my many years of being an athlete and a coach for athletes, and hundreds of people looking to change their lives both physically and mentally, I have realized that no matter how many tools you're given or how many people want greatness for you, it is something that only YOU can want for yourself. There are too many hours spent alone in your own brain to carry on through tough times without that person being the driving force. You can be your own worst enemy if you don't learn what it takes to succeed inside your own mind.

Some people think that this means finding a distinct reason for doing what you want to do, but for me it's not any one distinct reason, usually it's a combination of reasons, and that combination is the multiple past failures that someone thinks is their destiny to have to live with forever; it's not. No one is stuck unless they choose to stick there themselves. You do not need any outside driving force or persons granting you permission to go after your dream life, just the knowledge that you can do amazing things with the right work ethic moving forward in life. For me it has nothing to do with approval or disapproval of others. I only do it for me, although I know it will help others, it's selfishly for me, because what if a person who gave you drive by not believing in you all of sudden gives you their blessing, then where does the drive come from? It shouldn't be about proving others wrong, or searching for their approval, it's about your internal fire. Do you have the drive to work in humble silence to achieve what you want for your own internal benefit? Once the answer to that question is a yes for you, then you'll be on your way in the right direction. Because when you fully trust someone, it doesn't matter what someone says about him, because you KNOW in your heart what that person would or wouldn't do. The same can be true of yourself, when someone says you can't accomplish it.

Let's be real, people usually are affected by outside sources and others perceptions of them. Why else do we dress up nice, buy nice things, smell nice, etc.? It's O.K; it's how our world works. Use that to your advantage by knowing what goes on outside of your head, so that you can be more aware and focused inside of your head on the fact that none of it REALLY matters, because when you change the way you look at things, the things you look at change.

So how do "I" do it? I've reflected upon what it was that made me view the world the way I did, why am I so very happy, why I work so hard, how I achieve the things I do against all odds, and most importantly, how can I help others do the exact same. There is a famous quote by Abraham Lincoln that is one of the most fitting I can think of for the answer:

"Things may come to those who wait, but only the things left behind by those who hustle." – Abe Lincoln

My perspective on life and everything involved changed at a young age. When I decided I wanted to be great it wasn't just an idea, it was a driving, rooted, purpose within my being. It wasn't that I wanted to be great at one specific task; I wanted to be great at everything I did, every time I did it. Was it hard? HELL YES! But it was beyond worth it for me. I knew that at every misstep I could easily step back, give up, or quit and no one would blame me. Sadly it's because they aren't in the same pursuit of great that I am. I found that the only time to test my resolve to be great was in the midst of the fire, where I was being forged every time I entered it; to come out the man that I am today. I have an ability to take that horrible fearful feeling in the bottom of my stomach and use it as fuel to succeed; because I know what stands on the other side of that pain is greatness.

I am a friend of success ONLY because I am a not a stranger to fear, pain, and failures in life. I knew that I had to endure the hardships of my life by not backing out of my problems and failing to learn the valuable lessons hidden inside of them. It is a gift that I was given and a tool that I have earned through more literal blood, sweat, and tears than most people are capable of handling in their entire lifetime.

When I look back on my life I realize that I have come to a point where I am able to share these gifts with others now, in full confidence of helping them achieve great things in their lives as well. This is why I know so very deep in my soul that it is my calling to lead a life in service of others by helping them realize what great fires they have inside of them just waiting to be lit to burn like an inferno. I just wanted to have a happy life with my family and I was willing to WORK my tail off for it. Average is not in my vocabulary because average didn't get me where I am, and average is sure as heck not going to get me where I want to be in helping the people of the world who need to hear my message.

Inside of you there is a flame just waiting to be sparked and fueled to burn as bright as the sun once you are able to dig deep inside of yourself and find it. My life is a complete testament to that true statement. I was given far less tools to become who I am than so many other people born into this world. The difference for me is that I figured out what it meant to TRUST YOUR HUSTLE and I have carried the belief in myself to levels that even I never thought I would be capable of.

This is a message I want to share with the world because I want to accomplish a goal I will never get to experience if done correctly... I want to have a massive funeral because of all the people's lives I have touched along the way of my "dash" in life; Morbid yes, but so very true.

If you learn nothing else from this story of my life forged by fire, learn this. That as I write these last few lines of my autobiography on what would have been my 8th wedding anniversary on March 31st 2014, sitting next to my happy, smart, and healthy 9 year-old son on a couch in my home, while my twins are sound asleep in their beds upstairs, I would have never foreseen this reality to be mine as little as 16 years ago. I made a decision in my life to be great and I stuck to it with all my might, even when I could have veered from it so very easily. I applied a perspective that every person on this earth can apply by knowing that no matter what was thrown at me, I held the power to work in the right direction. I did not know how happy I would be by this time in my life, but I didn't have to know in order to work towards it. My faith directed me in ways I would have never known possible and it was all due to my unwavering dedication to a great work ethic, even when I didn't know if my hard work would pan out for the best.

So decide for yourself that this moment can and will be your deciding moment to be great in life at whatever it is you choose. Decide that you want something more than you know how to explain in words. Then put in more work than you were ready to put in, because that's what it's going to take. Your level of hard work may be far below the actual work necessary to achieve your state of happiness, but it DOES NOT mean that you cannot achieve it. All it means is that you are going to work harder than you have ever known to get something you have never had...Sound familiar? It should because that's the only way great things are earned and achieved in life, by doing something you haven't done before.

The truth is that you'll be in the top percentage of human beings when you do get there, because everyone reaches the level you will get to, but almost everyone stops there. When you get there and push forward you'll be above the crowd, because the road to success is a clean and barren road due to the fact that it's the road less traveled.

In life you will have many setbacks and pitfalls, but always remember when all else fails and there's nothing left, you can always TRUST YOUR HUSTLE!

TRUST YOUR HUSTLE:

A MESSAGE FROM ANTHONY

I want to personally thank you for taking the time to read my story and I genuinely hope you enjoyed it. I mostly hope you were able to pull something from it to take on your journey that can improve even one second of your life. I spent many years of my life hiding behind my hardships and keeping my story a secret, until I found that it was actually a source of strength for others to hear it. So I decided to share my story in hopes that you will learn something from it.

I hope you can find the strength to share your own inner most faults to feel the freedom of self I have learned to embrace. I hope you find a light at the end of your tunnel that can give you a glimmer of hope in a dark world. There are more than enough negative stories and hard times being shown in the media and in peoples lives daily, but for every bad story there exists a good one. With that in mind, when bad things happen to you it does not mean that you cannot change your view and create your own good from the bad. You simply have to realize one thing that I learned so many years ago.

When I think back to absolutely any hard time in my life, no matter its severity, one thing was a fact. I can remember a time afterwards where I was full of joy and happiness. Some times it would be a day after or months later, but that day DID come. So I always remind myself that although I may be in the midst of a trial in my life, there will be a day that comes soon where I will have an ear to ear smile and let out a laugh that shakes the negativity from my bones. I want you to carry that same thought with you any time you are in the middle of a rough patch. Remember back to a time of pain followed by a distinct memory of joy. Then make sure every choice you make from that moment forward is directed towards placing that smile on your face again, realizing that it wont be easy, but it will surely be worth it.

Thank you from the deepest part of my soul, and God Bless You!

INVITE ANTHONY

TRUCKS TO SPEAK

To invite Anthony to speak,

Please email Contact@AnthonyTrucks.com or call 925-756-7321

www.AnthonyTrucks.com

SERVICES

Speaking

Whether you're looking for a corporate keynote, fitness keynote, or a customized keynote specific to your company or organization, Anthony Trucks will deliver a world-class speech and experience for all in attendance. From his unique perspective, speech delivery, and life experiences, Anthony will create and deliver a speech that reaches your attendees in a way that will leave their hearts forever changed. Topics include athlete training, character development, productivity, empowerment, student engagement, and inclusion.

Corporate Coaching / Training

The quickest way to become the best is to be coached by the best. The world of business is becoming more personal as the world gets "smaller" with technology. Anthony's unique approach to coaching and training your staff will bring your company into the forefront of this ever changing world by focusing on communication, productivity, personal/team development, and leadership. So, if you want to bring yourself or your organization to the top ranks in personal achievement and income, contact Anthony Trucks today.

Consulting

Anthony Trucks' heart is rooted in the complete development and success of his clients. Many companies and organizations are coasting by "lifeless" and in need a jump-start to bring to life a brand or culture that is on life support. With Anthony Trucks Industries step-by-step consulting programs your organization can be reborn and live a new life full of boundless opportunity and success. Ready the crash cart and give your company the shock it needs to regain its strong heartbeat.

SOCIAL MEDIA

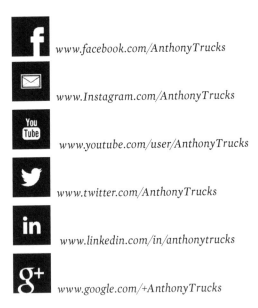

www.facebook.com/AnthonyTrucks

www.Instagram.com/AnthonyTrucks

www.youtube.com/user/AnthonyTrucks

www.twitter.com/AnthonyTrucks

www.linkedin.com/in/anthonytrucks

www.google.com/+AnthonyTrucks

Keep an eye out for **TRUST YOUR HUSTLE Pt. 2**: Light the fire
within to set your life ablaze

Made in the USA
Lexington, KY
14 November 2014